At Issue

What Role Should the U.S. Play in the Middle East?

Other Books in the At Issue Series:

At Issue

What Role Should the U.S. Play in the Middle East?

Noah Berlatsky, Book Editor

GREENHAVEN PRESS
A part of Gale, Cengage Learning

GALE
CENGAGE Learning

Detroit • New York • San Francisco • New Haven, Conn • Waterville, Maine • London

Christine Nasso, *Publisher*
Elizabeth Des Chenes, *Managing Editor*

© 2009 Greenhaven Press, a part of Gale, Cengage Learning.

Gale and Greenhaven Press are registered trademarks used herein under license.

For more information, contact:
Greenhaven Press
27500 Drake Rd.
Farmington Hills, MI 48331-3535
Or you can visit our Internet site at gale.cengage.com

For product information and technology assistance, contact us at

Gale Customer Support, 1-800-877-4253
For permission to use material from this text or product, submit all requests online at www.cengage.com/permissions

Further permissions questions can be emailed to permissionrequest@cengage.com

Articles in Greenhaven Press anthologies are often edited for length to meet page require-ments. In addition, original titles of these works are changed to clearly present the main thesis and to explicitly indicate the author's opinion. Every effort is made to ensure that Greenhaven Press accurately reflects the original intent of the authors. Every effort has been made to trace the owners of copyrighted material.

Cover photograph © Images.com/Corbis.

LIBRARY OF CONGRESS CATALOGING-IN-PUBLICATION DATA

What role should the U.S. play in the Middle East? / Noah Berlatsky, book editor.
      p. cm. -- (At issue)
   Includes bibliographical references and index.
   ISBN 978-0-7377-4450-7 (hardcover)
   ISBN 978-0-7377-4451-4 (pbk.)
   1. United States--Foreign relations--Middle East. 2. Middle East--Foreign relations--United States. I. Berlatsky, Noah.
   JZ1480.A55W53 2009
   327.73056--dc22
                                                                    2009006077

Printed in the United States of America
1 2 3 4 5 6 7 13 12 11 10 09

Contents

Introduction

Before discussing the question of what role the United States should play in the Middle East, it must first be asked whether the United States should play any role at all in that region. After all, the Middle East shares no border with the United States. In fact, it is thousands of miles away. And yet the Middle East has long been and remains one of America's central foreign policy concerns.

Scholars, policy makers, and commentators have approached the issue of U.S. involvement in the Middle East from a variety of perspectives, many of which can be seen as adhering to one of two philosophies. The first evaluates American foreign policy on the basis of practical interests: the United States should become involved in the Middle East if it helps America and should stay away if it does not. The second evaluates American foreign policy on the basis of morality: the United States should become involved in the Middle East if doing so is morally right and should not if it is morally wrong.

The first of these approaches—foreign policy based on American interests—is sometimes referred to as *realpolitik*. It is often associated with Henry Kissinger, the secretary of state in President Richard Nixon's administration. In his memoirs, Kissinger writes, "The United States ... must temper its missionary spirit with a concept of national interest." In other words, America needs to do what is best for America, rather than trying to save the rest of the world.

Some experts have argued that certain kinds of involvement in the Middle East have been in America's interests for various reasons. For instance, conservative commentator Stanley Kurtz, writing for the *National Review Online* on September 16, 2002, argued that the United States should invade Iraq "to stop Saddam Hussein from passing weapons of mass destruction to terrorists who will use them against the United

States." That is a realpolitik argument; Kurtz is saying the invasion is in the U.S. interest—it will protect the United States from harm in the future.

On the other hand, some experts have argued that involvement in the Middle East has worked against American interest. For example, British journalist and columnist Lindsey Hilsum, writing in the *New Statesman* on November 21, 2005, argued that invading Iraq destabilized that country and increased the terrorism danger to the West. "Realpolitik," Hilsum writes, "would have meant leaving Saddam in power. . . . Saddam Hussein is bad, but anarchy is worse." In other words, though Saddam Hussein was an evil dictator, leaving him in power was safer for America. Therefore, America should not have intervened to remove him.

The opposite of realpolitik is a moral or ideological approach. From this perspective, America should base its foreign policy on moral principles, like human rights, humanitarian aid, or democracy. Or, as the subhead of a *Wall Street Journal* editorial stated on June 1, 2001, "American policy should be based on American ideals."

Some experts have argued that morality demands U.S. intervention in the Middle East in certain situations. For example, Richard Land, a Christian evangelical leader and ethicist, argued in 2002 that in invading Iraq, America's "goal is not to conquer and subjugate the Iraqi people. Our goal is to remove a really atrocious, war-crimes-committing dictator who terrorizes and enslaves his own people." For Land, in other words, intervention was necessary on moral grounds.

Some commentators, however, have stated that the moral approach to the Middle East would have meant *not* intervening. For example, in his blog Once Upon a Time, writer Arthur Silber argued on June 17, 2006, that the United States should not have invaded Iraq because "Iraq constituted no threat to us, and our leaders knew it. Therefore, our invasion and occupation of Iraq were and are naked acts of aggression."

Silber's view is that the United States should not have invaded Iraq because doing so was immoral.

Realpolitik and moral perspectives are not always opposed to one another. In fact, they are often combined. For instance, in an address in November 2003, President George W. Bush said, "As long as the Middle East remains a place where freedom does not flourish, it will remain a place of stagnation, resentment, and violence ready for export." Thus, for Bush, intervening to establish democracy in the Middle East (a moral goal) will also reduce resentment, and thus reduce terrorist violence against America (a realpolitik goal).

Similarly, in a November 27, 2005, interview on the Web site of Al Jazeera, the chief Arabic-language news outlet, former U.S. Army intelligence officer David Dionisi said, "People in the Muslim world are not fighting us because of our freedoms or elections but our foreign policy. . . . The basic principle is: if you hurt someone, they're going to want to hurt you." Dionisi's view is that American foreign policy is harmful to those in the Middle East (a moral concern), resulting in violence that endangers American security (a realpolitik concern).

Whether in opposition to each other or in conjunction, realpolitik and morality are the lenses through which most commentators view foreign policy. The authors of the following viewpoints offer a range of perspectives on the role the United States should play in the Middle East, highlighting the importance and complexity of the issue.

1

U.S. Support of Repressive Regimes in the Middle East Encourages Terrorism

Stephen Zunes

Stephen Zunes is a professor of politics and international studies at the University of San Francisco. He is associate editor of Peace Review *and a foreign affairs columnist for the* National Catholic Reporter. *His latest book, coauthored with Jacob Mundy, is* Western Sahara: Nationalism and Conflict in Northwest Africa, *forthcoming from Syracuse University Press.*

The United States supports undemocratic governments in the Middle East such as Saudi Arabia. It also downplays human rights violations by its allies, such as Israel and (at one time) Iraq. Western critics sometimes claim that Arab peoples do not understand or want democracy. In fact, Middle Eastern peoples do want self-determination, and they resent that the United States supports injustice and oppression. This resentment fuels anti-American rhetoric, Muslim extremism, and terrorism.

More than forty years ago, President John F. Kennedy observed that "Those who make peaceful evolution impossible will make violent revolution inevitable." Despite disastrous consequences from ignoring this advice in the subsequent decades of the Cold War in such regions as Southeast Asia, Latin America and Africa, American policy makers may now be making the same tragic mistake in the Middle East. In aiding and abetting political repression, the United States has helped create the very forces that now threaten American security. Though U.S. support for repressive governments has widespread bipartisan support in Washington, history has shown repeatedly that such policies end up being counter to American interests over the long term.

The standard reason given by U.S. officials and many pundits in the American media for what motivated the attacks of September 11, 2001 is the terrorists' hatred of liberty and of democracy. According to President George W. Bush, "They hate . . . democratically elected government. They hate our freedoms—our freedom of religion, our freedom of speech, our freedom to vote and assemble and disagree with each other." Though Americans have reason to be proud of their country's democratic institutions and individual liberties, the unfortunate reality is that U.S. policy in the Middle East has tended not to promote freedom, but to support authoritarian governments and occupation armies. The contradiction between the democratic ideals with which most Americans identify and the perceived exigencies of superpower status is certainly not unique to current U.S. policy in the Middle East, yet its significance is rarely appreciated.

Attention to human rights by successive American administrations has always been relative to the perceived strategic importance of the country in question: the more important an allied regime is strategically, the less attention is given to human rights. Unfortunately for people living under the rule of Middle Eastern governments allied to the United States, their location makes their countries of great strategic value in the view of American policy makers. There is a price to pay for such priorities, however.

Repression Breeds Terror

Terrorism rarely rises out of democratic societies. When it does, terrorist groups are usually suppressed fairly easily, since few people agree with the terrorists' assertion that armed resistance is the best way to force needed political changes, especially when the targets are non-combatants. By contrast, it is no coincidence that political movements dedicated to advancing their cause through violence tend to arise within countries where governments hold power through violence. The United States plays a major role in propping up repressive governments which, in turn, has led to a terrorist backlash. Most Middle Easterners do not see American democracy at work, but they do see "Made in USA" on tear gas canisters and bomb casings used against civilians.

There is a tragic convenience to an American policy that strengthens ... repressive Arab regimes ... only to then claim that the lack of freedom in these countries is evidence that their people do not really want it.

For example, the autocratic regime in Saudi Arabia maintains its grip on power in part through the Saudi National Guard (SANG), which has been accused of widespread human rights abuses against suspected opponents. SANG, whose primary function is internal security, is almost entirely armed, trained and managed by the United States, largely through a network of military contractors. It may be no coincidence that what many believe to be Al-Qaeda's first terrorist attack, a November 1995 bombing that killed five American servicemen, was targeted at a U.S.-operated SANG training center in Riyadh.

Barely a month after the September 11 attacks, Great Britain's prestigious *Financial Times* observed, "For a long time after the Gulf War, the U.S. assumed its allies in the region—most of which are authoritarian regimes—could impose their views on their people. The error of this approach has become apparent."

Middle Eastern People Want Democracy

Many Americans question whether democracy is even possible in the Middle East, believing that human rights abuses are the inevitable outgrowth of authoritarian forms of government that are required and reinforced by cultural norms. Attitudes underlying these questions minimize the importance of democracy and human rights to Middle Eastern peoples and the desire of Middle Eastern peoples to encourage democratization and improve the human rights records of their governments. Such American assumptions at times harbor somewhat racist overtones. For example, widespread misunderstandings in the West of Islamic principles regarding human rights have minimized popular sympathy with victims of human rights abuses in many of these countries. A crude kind of structural-functionalism [social theory that emphasizes the stability of cultures] and pseudo-sensitivity appears to underline the belief that the lack of better human rights records by Middle Eastern governments is somehow a cultural phenomenon that no policy shift by the United States could alter. Even some otherwise reputable scholars, such as Harvard University's Samuel Huntington, will go to some lengths to dismiss the potential for democracy in the Islamic world. It is not inaccurate to generalize that there has tended to be a greater tolerance for autocratic rule and a lesser emphasis on individual liberties in the Islamic world than in the West. However, there is also a strong belief in a social contract between ruler and subject that gives the people the right to resist if the rule is unjust. Furthermore, international human rights covenants routinely violated by Middle Eastern governments are based upon the Universal Declaration of Human Rights, deemed universal because it does reflect an international consensus. Given that most Middle Eastern governments have signed the International Covenant on Civil and Political Rights, which is based upon the Universal Declaration, these governments are legally bound to uphold its principles. Furthermore, individual Arabs and Muslims do not like being detained, denied due process, tortured and murdered for their political beliefs by repressive governments anymore than do their Western Christian and Jewish counterparts.

Even though democracy and individual liberty is not common in the Arab-Islamic world, the emphasis in the West on cultural or religious explanations tends to minimize other factors that are arguably more salient. These include the legacy of colonialism, high levels of militarization, and uneven economic development, much of which can be linked in no small part to the policies of Western governments, including the United States. There is a tragic convenience to an American policy that strengthens the police and military of repressive Arab regimes, better enabling them to crush incipient human rights movements, only to then claim that the lack of freedom in these countries is evidence that their people do not really want it. . . . These arms transfers and the diplomatic and economic support systems provided by the United States play an important role in keeping these regimes in power by strengthening the hand of the state and supporting internal repression.

A further irony is that American political leaders then use the dictatorial orientation of these Arab regimes as an excuse for supporting the government of Israel, which also suppresses Arab peoples demanding democracy and human rights. Domestic political groups in the United States allied with Israel—along with sympathetic individuals in politics, academia, and the media—have frequently played upon stereotypes of the "authoritarian nature" of Arab societies as reasons why the United States should continue large-scale military and economic support of the Israeli government. Egyptian human rights activist Hafez Abu Saada expressed the sentiment of many Arab democrats when he noted the implicit racism in a U.S. that believes in "Democracy for the Jews, but not for the Arabs." . . .

A Double Standard

In other parts of the world, even where there may have been widespread repression, the United States has insisted that competitive elections and other legal structures are an adequate indicator of democracy. This is why even in the case of El Salvador in the 1980s—where, despite formal competitive elections, government-backed death squads murdered tens of thousands of dissidents—the country was labeled a "democracy" by the U.S. government and much of the American media. The Middle East is more problematic, however, since some of America's closest allies are absolute monarchies without even the pretense of democratic institutions. As a result, successive administrations and the media have frequently labeled such governments as "moderate," even if there was nothing particularly moderate in their level of despotism. The term is used primarily in reference to governments that have been friendly to the United States and its foreign policy goals in the Middle East; it has also been used in reference to governments that have been relatively less hostile towards Israel and U.S.-led peace initiatives. In either case, there is virtually no correlation between this label and a given government's record on democracy and human rights. This is how Saudi Arabia, a fundamentalist and misogynist theocracy that engages in widespread human rights abuses, is labeled so frequently in the United States as a "moderate" Arab regime.

Unlike Saudi Arabia, most Middle Eastern states do have elections. They are usually formalities, however, the primary purpose of which is to ratify the existing leadership. The smaller emirates of the Persian Gulf, that generally eschew any kind of formal elections, traditionally maintained legitimacy through the *majlis* system, which provides for the direct petitioning of grievances to royalty. In addition, monarchical succession was not automatic to the eldest son or any single member of the royal family; the successor was chosen by a consensus of tribal elders based on his qualifications. It was the British, who dominated the Gulf region during the nine-teenth and twentieth centuries, that helped ossify the sheikly system to a largely inherited position. With the addition of strong American backing in subsequent years, several of these Arab monarchies have evolved from their relatively open traditional tribal governing structures to ones more closely resembling modern bureaucratic authoritarianism. As a result, human rights abuses have increased in a number of these countries and the legitimacy of these governments is being challenged to a growing degree from within. Popular resentment cannot help but expand beyond the regime in question to its chief foreign patron as well.

As with other parts of the world, the U.S. government will often downplay the human rights abuses of its allies and exaggerate the abuses of its adversaries. To cite some recent examples: in the State Department's annual human rights report, the description of the Sultanate of Oman was changed, as a result of pressure from department superiors, to downplay the authoritarian nature of the regime. For example, in the 1991 report, Oman is described as "an absolute monarchy;" a more recent report simply refers to the sultanate as "a monarchy without popularly elected representative institutions." More recently, the 2000 human rights report noted how Egypt's military courts "do not ensure civilian defendants due process before an independent tribunal." However, thanks to pressure from above, all references to these unfair tribunals were dropped from the 2001 report even though they continue. The State Department has even allowed Israeli officials to review and edit its human rights report on Israeli practices in the occupied territories prior to publication, substantially toning down the original analysis. Even Iraq had its lack of democracy and poor human rights record downplayed by U.S. officials during its invasion of Iran in the 1980s. Only after its invasion of Kuwait in 1990 was the record corrected and Iraq's violations prominently exposed.

Shunning Democracies

Rather than encourage democratization in the Middle East, the United States has reduced—or maintained at low levels—its economic, military, and diplomatic support of Arab countries that have experienced substantial liberalization in recent years. For example, Jordan received large-scale U.S. support in the 1970s and 1980s despite widespread repression and authoritarian rule. In the early 1990s, when it became perhaps the most democratic country in the Arab world—with a relatively free press, opposition political parties, and lively debate in a parliament that wielded real political power within a constitutional monarchy—the United States suspended foreign aid. Similarly, aid to Yemen was cut off within months of the newly reunified country's first democratic election in 1990. The official explanation for the cutoff of U.S. support for these two countries was because of their failure to support the United States in its war against Iraq. However, the reason these governments could not back the American war effort was because their leaders—unlike those of their more autocratic Arab neighbors that supported the war—needed to be responsive to their citizenry, who generally opposed the war, *because* they had relatively open political systems. By contrast, American support for dictatorial regimes—such as Egypt, Saudi Arabia and the smaller Gulf emirates that backed the U.S.-led war effort—increased during this period.

As *Newsweek* magazine observed, in reference to Pakistan, "It may be a good thing that Pakistan is ruled by a friendly military dictator rather than what could well be a hostile democracy." As British journalist Robert Fisk noted, "Far better to have a [Egyptian president Hosni] Mubarak or a King Abdullah [of Saudi Arabia] or a King Fahd [of Saudi Arabia] running the show than to let the Arabs vote for a real government that might oppose U.S. policies in the region." . . .

Fuel for Radical Islam

In recent years, the United States has rationalized its support for autocratic regimes in the Middle East, North Africa and Central Asia as a regrettable but necessary means of suppressing the Islamic opposition. In many respects, this policy closely parallels the decades of support during the Cold War of repressive right-wing governments in the name of anti-Communism. The result is similar, however: the lack of open political expression only encourages large segments of the oppressed populations to ally with an underground—and often violent and authoritarian—opposition movement. In Islamic countries, that often means extremist Islamic groups. As Hafez Abu Saada, secretary general of the Egyptian Organization for Human Rights said, "Politics is prohibited in this society in general, but the government can't close the mosque." Furthermore, the lack of a free press means that for many Muslims who do not believe the official media, the only alternative source of information comes through the Internet and other anonymous alternative sources, exposing them to extremist propaganda, including conspiracy theories, without any credible countervailing sources of information.

Self-righteous claims by American leaders that the anger expressed by Arabs and Muslims towards the United States is because of "our commitment to freedom" only exacerbates feelings of ill-will and feeds the rage manifested in anti-American violence and terrorism.

Rather than disliking American democracy, most Middle Easterners are envious of it and are resentful that the American attitude seems to be that they are somehow not deserving of it. The anti-terrorist coalition the United States has built for its military response to the September 2001 attacks— centered around alliances with the absolute monarchy in Saudi Arabia, the military regime of Pakistan and the crypto-

Communists that rule Uzbekistan—has been labeled "Operation Enduring Freedom." It's an irony lost on few Middle Easterners. . . .

U.S. Support of Repression

To those in the Arab and Islamic world, U.S. defense of Israeli repression against their Palestinian brethren is perhaps the most sensitive of a whole series of grievances regarding American callousness towards internationally-recognized human rights in the Middle East. Yet it is the U.S. support of repression by regimes of Islamic countries that Muslims know the best. Morocco and Turkey, like Israel, have utilized American weapons in the occupation and repression of other peoples. Uzbekistan, Saudi Arabia, Egypt and other Islamic countries have suffered under autocratic rule maintained, in varying degrees, through American military, economic and diplomatic support.

In a major White House speech on U.S. policy towards the Israeli-Palestinian conflict in June 2002, President [George W.] Bush insisted that democratic governance and an end to violence and corruption must be a prerequisite for Palestinian independence. This came across as particularly ironic, given that his administration—as well as previous administrations—has so strongly supported a series of violent, corrupt and autocratic regimes throughout the Middle East and beyond. Millions of people watched the president of the United States demand that the Palestinians create a democratic political system based upon "tolerance and liberty" while at the same time befriending other Middle Eastern governments that are among the most intolerant and autocratic regimes in the world. It was ironic that President Bush specifically criticized the Palestinian Authority's lack of a fair judicial system. It was the same infamous State Security Court he criticized, which has carried out some of the worst human rights abuses, that was established with strong U.S. support and was once praised by Vice President Al Gore when he visited Jericho in 1994.

Until the extent of the repression and the American complicity in the repression is recognized, it will be difficult to understand the negative sentiments a growing number of ordinary people in the Islamic world have towards the United States. Therefore, self-righteous claims by American leaders that the anger expressed by Arabs and Muslims towards the United States is because of "our commitment to freedom" only exacerbates feelings of ill-will and feeds the rage manifested in anti-American violence and terrorism.

2

U.S. Intervention Will Encourage Democracy in the Middle East

George W. Bush

George W. Bush is the forty-third president of the United States.

The United States should not retreat into isolationism but instead should spread freedom throughout the world. Radical Islam opposes freedom in the Middle East and abroad. It should be confronted and defeated. There has been dramatic progress toward stability and democracy in Iraq and Afghanistan. For the U.S. to withdraw from these countries before the violence there is subdued would grant control of them to terrorists. America should also encourage democraticization in Saudi Arabia, Egypt, and especially in the repressive nation of Iran.

In this decisive year [of 2006], you and I will make choices that determine both the future and the character of our country. We will choose to act confidently in pursuing the enemies of freedom—or retreat from our duties in the hope of an easier life. We will choose to build our prosperity by leading the world economy—or shut ourselves off from trade and opportunity. In a complex and challenging time, the road of isolationism and protectionism may seem broad and inviting—yet it ends in danger and decline. The only way to protect our people, the only way to secure the peace, the only way to control our destiny is by our leadership—so the United States of America will continue to lead.

George W. Bush, "State of the Union Address by the President of the United States," whitehouse.gov, January 31, 2006.

Abroad, our nation is committed to an historic, long-term goal—we seek the end of tyranny in our world. Some dismiss that goal as misguided idealism. In reality, the future security of America depends on it. On September the 11th, 2001, we found that problems originating in a failed and oppressive state 7,000 miles away [Afghanistan] could bring murder and destruction to our country. Dictatorships shelter terrorists, and feed resentment and radicalism, and seek weapons of mass destruction. Democracies replace resentment with hope, respect the rights of their citizens and their neighbors, and join the fight against terror. Every step toward freedom in the world makes our country safer—so we will act boldly in freedom's cause.

Far from being a hopeless dream, the advance of freedom is the great story of our time. In 1945, there were about two dozen lonely democracies in the world. Today, there are 122. And we're writing a new chapter in the story of self-government—with women lining up to vote in Afghanistan, and millions of Iraqis marking their liberty with purple ink, and men and women from Lebanon to Egypt debating the rights of individuals and the necessity of freedom. At the start of 2006, more than half the people of our world live in democratic nations. And we do not forget the other half—in places like Syria and Burma, Zimbabwe, North Korea, and Iran—because the demands of justice, and the peace of this world, require their freedom, as well.

America rejects the false comfort of isolationsim.

Radical Islam Opposes Freedom

No one can deny the success of freedom, but some men rage and fight against it. And one of the main sources of reaction and opposition is radical Islam—the perversion by a few of a noble faith into an ideology of terror and death. Terrorists like

[Osama] bin Laden are serious about mass murder—and all of us must take their declared intentions seriously. They seek to impose a heartless system of totalitarian control throughout the Middle East, and arm themselves with weapons of mass murder.

Their aim is to seize power in Iraq, and use it as a safe haven to launch attacks against America and the world. Lacking the military strength to challenge us directly, the terrorists have chosen the weapon of fear. When they murder children at a school in Beslan [Russia] or blow up commuters in London [England] or behead a bound captive, the terrorists hope these horrors will break our will, allowing the violent to inherit the earth. But they have miscalculated: We love our freedom, and we will fight to keep it.

We Must Fight the Terrorists

In a time of testing, we cannot find security by abandoning our commitments and retreating within our borders. If we were to leave these vicious attackers alone, they would not leave us alone. They would simply move the battlefield to our own shores. There is no peace in retreat. And there is no honor in retreat. By allowing radical Islam to work its will—by leaving an assaulted world to fend for itself—we would signal to all that we no longer believe in our own ideals, or even in our own courage. But our enemies and our friends can be certain: The United States will not retreat from the world, and we will never surrender to evil.

America rejects the false comfort of isolationism. We are the nation that saved liberty in Europe, and liberated death camps, and helped raise up democracies, and faced down an evil empire. Once again, we accept the call of history to deliver the oppressed and move this world toward peace. We remain on the offensive against terror networks. We have killed or captured many of their leaders—and for the others, their day will come.

We remain on the offensive in Afghanistan, where a fine President and a National Assembly are fighting terror while building the institutions of a new democracy. We're on the offensive in Iraq, with a clear plan for victory. First, we're helping Iraqis build an inclusive government, so that old resentments will be eased and the insurgency will be marginalized.

Second, we're continuing reconstruction efforts, and helping the Iraqi government to fight corruption and build a modern economy, so all Iraqis can experience the benefits of freedom. And, third, we're striking terrorist targets while we train Iraqi forces that are increasingly capable of defeating the enemy. Iraqis are showing their courage every day, and we are proud to be their allies in the cause of freedom.

Progress in Iraq

Our work in Iraq is difficult because our enemy is brutal. But that brutality has not stopped the dramatic progress of a new democracy. In less than three years, the nation has gone from dictatorship to liberation, to sovereignty, to a constitution, to national elections. At the same time, our coalition has been relentless in shutting off terrorist infiltration, clearing out insurgent strongholds, and turning over territory to Iraqi security forces. I am confident in our plan for victory; I am confident in the will of the Iraqi people; I am confident in the skill and spirit of our military. Fellow citizens, we are in this fight to win, and we are winning.

The road of victory is the road that will take our troops home. As we make progress on the ground, and Iraqi forces increasingly take the lead, we should be able to further decrease our troop levels—but those decisions will be made by our military commanders, not by politicians in Washington, D.C.

Our coalition has learned from our experience in Iraq. We've adjusted our military tactics and changed our approach to reconstruction. Along the way, we have benefitted from responsible criticism and counsel offered by members of Congress of both parties. In the coming year, I will continue to reach out and seek your good advice. Yet, there is a difference between responsible criticism that aims for success, and defeatism that refuses to acknowledge anything but failure. Hindsight alone is not wisdom, and second-guessing is not a strategy.

We Must Not Withdraw from Iraq

With so much in the balance, those of us in public office have a duty to speak with candor. A sudden withdrawal of our forces from Iraq would abandon our Iraqi allies to death and prison, would put men like bin Laden and [terrorist Abu Musab al-] Zarqawi in charge of a strategic country, and show that a pledge from America means little. Members of Congress, however we feel about the decisions and debates of the past, our nation has only one option: We must keep our word, defeat our enemies, and stand behind the American military in this vital mission.

Liberty is the future of every nation in the Middle East, because liberty is the right and hope of all humanity.

Our men and women in uniform are making sacrifices—and showing a sense of duty stronger than all fear. They know what it's like to fight house to house in a maze of streets, to wear heavy gear in the desert heat, to see a comrade killed by a roadside bomb. And those who know the costs also know the stakes. Marine Staff Sergeant Dan Clay was killed last month fighting in Fallujah. He left behind a letter to his family, but his words could just as well be addressed to every American. Here is what Dan wrote: "I know what honor is. . . . It has been an honor to protect and serve all of you. I faced death with the secure knowledge that you would not have to. . . . Never falter! Don't hesitate to honor and support those of us who have the honor of protecting that which is worth protecting." . . .

Our nation is grateful to the fallen, who live in the memory of our country. We're grateful to all who volunteer to wear our nation's uniform—and as we honor our brave troops, let us never forget the sacrifices of America's military families.

Democracy Will Defeat Terror

Our offensive against terror involves more than military action. Ultimately, the only way to defeat the terrorists is to defeat their dark vision of hatred and fear by offering the hopeful alternative of political freedom and peaceful change. So the United States of America supports democratic reform across the broader Middle East. Elections are vital, but they are only the beginning. Raising up a democracy requires the rule of law, and protection of minorities, and strong, accountable institutions that last longer than a single vote.

The great people of Egypt have voted in a multi-party presidential election—and now their government should open paths of peaceful opposition that will reduce the appeal of radicalism. The Palestinian people have voted in elections. And now the leaders of [Palestinian militant Islamist political party] Hamas must recognize Israel, disarm, reject terrorism, and work for lasting peace. Saudi Arabia has taken the first steps of reform—now it can offer its people a better future by pressing forward with those efforts. Democracies in the Middle East will not look like our own, because they will reflect the traditions of their own citizens. Yet liberty is the future of every nation in the Middle East, because liberty is the right and hope of all humanity.

The same is true of Iran, a nation now held hostage by a small clerical elite that is isolating and repressing its people. The regime in that country sponsors terrorists in the Palestinian territories and in Lebanon—and that must come to an end. The Iranian government is defying the world with its nuclear ambitions, and the nations of the world must not permit the Iranian regime to gain nuclear weapons. America will continue to rally the world to confront these threats.

Tonight, let me speak directly to the citizens of Iran: America respects you, and we respect your country. We respect your right to choose your own future and win your own freedom. And our nation hopes one day to be the closest of friends with a free and democratic Iran.

3

The United States Needs to Cultivate Allies, Not Democracies

Flynt Leverett and Hillary Mann Leverett

Flynt Leverett has worked as a Middle East expert with the National Security Council, the State Department, and the CIA. He is currently a senior fellow and director of the Geopolitics of Energy Initiative of the New America Foundation. One of his most recent books is Dealing with Tehran: Assessing U.S. Diplomatic Options Toward Iran *(2006). Hillary Mann Leverett is a career Foreign Service officer, with primary expertise in the Middle East and Persian Gulf regions. She has worked at the National Security Council, with the U.S. Mission to the United Nations, and as special assistant to the U.S. ambassador to Egypt.*

The assassination in Pakistan of Benazir Bhutto, a political candidate favored by the United States, shows that the American goal of democraticization is flawed. The United States and its policies are not popular in the Middle East. For example, most Pakistanis do not support the U.S. war on terror. Therefore, democratically elected governments will not support the war on terror either. Instead of democraticization, the United States needs to provide better military and financial support to nondemocratic governments that oppose militant Islamists. In particular, the United States should more strongly back the undemocratic Pakistani president Perez Musharraf.

Flynt Leverett and Hillary Mann Leverett, "Most Dems no better than Bush on Pakistan," Salon.com, January 3, 2008. This article first appeared in Salon.com, at http://www.salon.com. An online version remains in the Salon archives. Reprinted with permission.

Last week [December 2007] the assassination of [Pakistani Opposition Political leader] Benazir Bhutto marked the failure of an ill-conceived U.S. attempt to orchestrate the return of a deeply divisive political exile, discredited by allegations of corruption and incompetence, to take power in Pakistan. The [George W.] Bush administration's aim was to install a leader who would simultaneously "democratize" and secularize her country, fight terrorist groups, and make peace with Israel. Instead, the sad event of Bhutto's murder has exposed the strategic bankruptcy of the administration's Pakistan policy. But Democrats should not feel vindicated by this failure, for they have endorsed virtually all of the Bush team's mistaken views about Pakistan policy.

One of President Bush's more appalling flights of fancy in the foreign policy arena is his belief that democratically elected governments will somehow be more inclined than incumbent authoritarians to support U.S. policy objectives that are wildly unpopular with their own electorates. The logical absurdity of this proposition should be readily apparent, but, nevertheless, the Bush administration has proceeded blithely to test it in the real world: In January 2006, the White House and Secretary of State Condoleezza Rice insisted, over the objections of Palestinian and Israeli leaders, on holding elections in occupied Palestinian territories—purportedly to elect a Palestinian government that would have the legitimacy to crack down on ongoing anti-Israeli violence. The result of this experiment, of course, was the victory of [militant Islamist party] Hamas, long designated by the United States as a terrorist organization.

A Foolhardy Course

Unfortunately, the Bush administration did not draw the appropriate lessons from this episode and decided to extend its second-term push for "democratization" in the Middle East to embrace Pakistan as well. But on-the-ground conditions in

Pakistan make any push for "free and fair" elections there a foolhardy course for U.S. policy. Polls indicate that the majority of Pakistan's population today is overwhelmingly opposed to many U.S. policy goals, including killing or capturing al-Qaida and Taliban affiliates and their Pakistani allies. In such an environment, any government produced by genuinely open elections will not be willing or able to support U.S. objectives in the war on terror. Nevertheless, the goal of democratizing Pakistan through presumptively "open" elections has been supported not only by the administration and other Republicans, but by the Democratic "opposition" as well (more on this below).

In 2002, President Pervez Musharraf allowed carefully controlled elections to be held in Pakistan. Those elections produced a relatively competent technocratic administration, including Shaukat Aziz, who was selected "finance minister of the year" by *Euromoney* and *The Banker* magazines. In 2004, Aziz became prime minister as well as finance minister; during his three years as Pakistan's head of government, he presided over the most sustained period of economic reform and modernization in the country's history. But Washington, in its bipartisan wisdom, said that this was not good enough.

The Bush administration coupled its support for Pakistan's democratization with an effort to handpick Benazir Bhutto as her country's democratic "savior." But we have also seen this (very bad) movie before in the administration's abortive effort to promote [discredited Iraqi politician] Ahmad Chalabi as the key to "democratizing" and stabilizing post-Saddam Iraq. Once again, the Bush administration turned to a Western-educated political exile, the head of a family kleptocracy [corrupt ruling group] who had twice shown herself to be an ineffective head of government, to shore up its tattered strategic partnership with Islamabad [Pakistan]. Like Chalabi, Bhutto played to all of Washington's preferences, saying that she would lead a renewed fight against the Taliban and al-Qaida in northwestern Pakistan (notwithstanding the fact that, as prime minister in 1993–1995, she authorized extensive Pakistani support for the emerging Taliban movement) and sending messages to Israeli leaders that she would recognize Israel.

Pakistan and Afghanistan Abandoned

In the aftermath of Bhutto's death, a conventional wisdom is already taking shape about America's Pakistan policy: that the Bush administration supported Musharraf for too long and too uncritically. Certainly, most Democratic presidential candidates and political leaders are making this charge. But the sad reality is that after Musharraf helped the United States in its post-9/11 campaign to unseat the Taliban in Afghanistan, the Bush administration effectively walked away from both Afghanistan and Pakistan, just as its predecessors did in the 1990s after a decade of extensive U.S.-Pakistani cooperation to support Afghan *mujahedin* [Muslim warriors] resisting the Soviet occupation of their country.

Clearly, the Bush administration failed to finish the job against either the Taliban or al-Qaida in Afghanistan when it had the chance. Indeed, in early 2002, the administration withdrew the critical special forces and paramilitary cadres that were spearheading the campaign to round up Taliban and al-Qaida elements in Afghanistan so that those forces could regroup, redeploy and begin "preparing the battlefield" for America's upcoming invasion of Iraq. Moreover, the administration failed to stabilize Afghanistan in the aftermath of the Taliban's overthrow [in 2001] and vetoed efforts by the international community to do so by blocking the expansion of the international Security Assistance Force outside Kabul until the security situation in the country had deteriorated to a dangerous point.

All this meant that post-Taliban Afghanistan became a much bigger security problem for Musharraf than would have been the case if the Bush administration's strategic decision making had not been so incompetent. This problem was exacerbated when Osama bin Laden and several senior associates took refuge in northwestern Pakistan in 2002—beyond the logistical and political capabilities of the Pakistani army to reach. That same year, the White House refused to fund serious counter-narcotics initiatives in Afghanistan to spray poppy fields or bomb processing facilities, thereby assuring that Musharraf's Taliban adversaries would have an independent and substantial source of funding.

Counterterrorism Bungled

Furthermore, while Washington worked with Afghanistan's neighbors to establish the [Hamid] Karzai government in December 2001, the Bush administration did not sustain the robust regional diplomatic effort that was needed to support Afghanistan's post-Taliban political reconstitution. Rather than build on the regional diplomacy that had launched the Karzai government and establish a regional framework for post-conflict stabilization in Afghanistan, the White House opted to pursue purely bilateral security arrangements with former Soviet states in Central Asia and with India. For Pakistan, this meant that support for the war on terror was no longer a broadly legitimated regional imperative, but a coercively imposed U.S. diktat [dictatorial command].

Musharraf's government represents the best hope for stability in Pakistan and Afghanistan.

And, while Washington demanded, with increasing stridency, that Islamabad move against Taliban and al-Qaida elements on Pakistani territory, the Bush administration and Congress could not get their act together to provide Musharraf with significant financial support until 2005. In this regard, statements that the United States has provided Musharraf with $10 billion in assistance since Sept. 11, 2001 are misleading. In fact, more than half of that amount is not true "assistance," but rather reimbursements for costs accrued by the Pakistani military supporting U.S. counterterrorism operations. With regard to the most significant channels of U.S. economic and security assistance to Pakistan, the Bush administration did not put together a meaningful aid package for Musharraf until 2003, and this package was not enacted into law until December 2004—more than three years after 9/11 and well after the United States had blown any real chance to destroy al-Qaida. (The same pattern applies to U.S. efforts to stem the narcotics trade in Afghanistan; the Bush administration did not begin to develop even a superficially coherent counter-narcotics strategy for Afghanistan until 2005—too late to break the critical financial link between the opium trade and the resurgent Taliban.)

Work With, Not Against Musharraf

In the wake of Bhutto's death, it is clear that the Bush administration has no Plan B for Pakistan. But Democrats—with the singular exception of presidential hopeful Sen. Chris Dodd—want to "double down" on the administration's failed approach, effectively pursuing Bush's "Bhutto strategy" without Bhutto. Thus, New Mexico Gov. Bill Richardson talks obtusely about organizing all of Pakistan's "democratic" parties into a coalition government, even though, if Pakistani politicians were capable of such a step, it would not need to be suggested by an American politician. Richardson also advocates withholding all military assistance to Pakistan until Musharraf steps down; similarly, Sen. Hillary Clinton talks vacuously about the lack of sufficient conditionality on U.S. assistance to Pakistan. Sen, Joseph Biden, for his part, talks about the need to proceed expeditiously to parliamentary elections. Biden anticipates, with seeming sincerity, that Bhutto's party, the PPP—now headed by her 19-year-old son, who will not be able to lead the party in the next round of elections, as this would interfere with his academic schedule as an Oxford undergraduate—would win the right to form the next government.

Sound policy toward Pakistan must start with a sober understanding of reality. That reality was described with admirable succinctness in 2004 by the 9/11 Commission, writing in its final report: "Musharraf's government represents the best hope for stability in Pakistan and Afghanistan." But insisting that Musharraf—or any potential successor from the senior ranks of the Pakistani army—break ranks with his military power base and the only institution that can limit the spread of militant violence in Pakistan and Afghanistan is only going to undermine the prospects for such stability.

Getting Pakistan "right" will require that we, first of all, get Afghanistan "right," and that we embed both of these troubled states in a broader regional strategy that includes the development of regional security institutions. Russia and China are already moving in this direction with their cultivation of the Shanghai Cooperation Organization, encompassing the former Soviet states of Central Asia—which have largely abandoned their post-9/11 security ties to the United States— and including Pakistan, India and Iran as observers. If the United States wants to preserve a serious leadership role in the region, or simply protect its critical security interests where Central and South Asia come together, it will need to abandon comforting illusions about "democratization" and begin working seriously to persuade Pakistan and other regional states that they can serve their interests best by working with us.

4

U.S. Dependence on Middle East Oil Undermines Democracy Building

Dr. Gal Luft

Dr. Gal Luft is one of America's leading experts on energy security. He is executive director of the Institute for the Analysis of Global Security (IAGS) and cofounder of the Set America Free Coalition.

Because of its reliance on Middle Eastern oil, the United States is often forced to choose between its humanitarian principles and its energy needs. U.S. payments for oil strengthen the region's undemocratic regimes, and often even end up in the hands of terrorist networks. When the United States does try to push for government reform in the region, Middle Eastern nations can simply turn to China and other growing nations happy to provide diplomatic support in return for energy. Finding new sources of oil, either abroad or domestically, is not a realistic solution to the problem, since experts predict that the Middle East's percentage of world oil supplies is going to grow. Instead, the United States must switch to alternative fuels, like ethanol, electricity, and coal.

As consumer of a quarter of the world's oil supply and holder of a mere three percent of global oil reserves the U.S. is heavily dependent on foreign oil, and a growing share

Dr. Gal Luft, "America's Oil Dependence and Its Implications for U.S. Middle East Policy," Testimony by Dr. Gal Luft Before the Senate Foreign Relations Subcommittee on Near Eastern and South Asian Affairs, October 20, 2005, pp. 1–6. Reproduced by permission of Gal Luft.

of this oil comes from the Persian Gulf. America's dependence on foreign oil has increased from 30 percent in 1973, when OPEC [Organization of Petroleum Exporting Countries] imposed its oil embargo, to 60 percent today. According to the Department of Energy this dependence is projected to reach 70 percent by 2025. In the wake of the war on terrorism, the rise of China and India and growing voices within the oil industry that "the era of easy oil is over," it has become apparent to many that America's oil policy is unsustainable and that such a policy subjects the nation to grave risks.

Since the 1945 meeting between President Franklin Roosevelt and King Abdul Aziz ibn Saud, the founder of the Saudi monarchy, U.S. foreign policy has been subservient to the nation's energy needs. Access to the Persian Gulf oil required robust and costly military presence in the region and frequent interventions. Worse, the U.S. has been forced to coddle some of the world's worst despots just because they held the key to our prosperity, hence compromising American values and principles.

Of the 11 million barrels per day (mbd) the U.S. imports today, close to 3mbd come from the Middle East. But in the years to come dependence on the Middle East is projected to increase by leaps and bounds. The reason is that reserves outside of the Middle East are being depleted at a much faster rate than those in the region. The overall reserves-to-production ratio—an indicator of how long proven reserves would last at current production rates—outside of the Middle East is about 15 years comparing to roughly 80 years in the Middle East. According to Exxon Corporation and PFC Energy, non-OPEC production, including Russia and West Africa will peak within a decade. At that point the amount of oil found outside of the Middle East will decline steeply, putting OPEC in the driver seat of the world economy.

These projections require that we take a sober, long-term look at the impact of our growing dependence on our strategic posture in the Middle East.

The Cost of Middle East Oil

Oil prices are not going down any time soon. The rise in oil prices will yield large financial surpluses to the Middle Eastern oil producers. This petrodollar windfall will strengthen the jihadists while undermining the strategic relationship the region's oil producers have with the U.S.

The U.S. [is] in an odd situation in which it is funding both sides in the war on terrorism.

As President [George W.] Bush said [in] April [2005], U.S. dependence on overseas oil is a "foreign tax on the American people." Indeed, oil imports constitute a quarter of the U.S. trade deficit and are a major contributor to the loss of jobs and investment opportunities. According to a study on the hidden cost of oil by the National Defense Council Foundation, the periodic oil shocks the U.S. has experienced since the 1973 Arab oil embargo cost the economy almost $2.5 trillion. More importantly, while the U.S. economy is bleeding, oil-producing nations increase their oil revenues dramatically to the detriment of our national security. The numbers speak for themselves: In November 2001, a barrel of oil was selling for $18. In less than four years the price jumped to $70. This means that Saudi Arabia, which exports about 10 mbd, receives an extra half billion dollars every day from consuming nations, and Iran, which exports 2.5 mbd, an extra $125 million. This windfall benefits the non-democratic governments of the Middle East and other producers and finds its way to the jihadists committed to America's destruction as petrodollars trickle their way through charities and government handouts to *madrassas* [Islamic schools] and mosques, as well as outright support of terrorist groups.

It is widely accepted that Saudi Arabia's oil wealth has directly enabled the spread of Wahhabism [extreme movement within Islam] around the world. The Saudis use oil funds to control most of the Arabic language media and are now moving to gain growing control over Western media. Only [recently] Saudi Prince Al-Waleed bin Talal, the world's fifth richest man, purchased 5.46 percent of Fox News corporation.

Petrodollars garnered from the U.S. and other countries are also being used by Saudi Arabia systematically to provide social services, build "Islamic centers" and schools, pay preachers' salaries and, in some cases, fund terror organizations. In July 2005 undersecretary of the Treasury Stuart Levey, testifying before the Senate Committee on Banking, Housing, and Urban Affairs, noted, "Wealthy Saudi financiers and charities have funded terrorist organizations and causes that support terrorism and the ideology that fuels the terrorists agenda. Even today, we believe that Saudi donors may still be a significant source of terrorist financing, including for the insurgency in Iraq."

The U.S. [is] in an odd situation in which it is funding both sides in the war on terrorism. We finance the defense of the Free World against its sworn enemies through our tax dollars. And at the same time we support hostile regimes through the transfer of petrodollars. If we don't change course we will bleed more dollars each year as our enemies gather strength. Steady increase in world demand for oil means further enrichment of the corrupt and dictatorial regimes in the Persian Gulf and continued access of terrorist groups to a viable financial network which allows them to remain a lethal threat to the U.S. and its allies.

The Coming War for Oil

The Middle East is gradually shifting from being a unipolar region in which the U.S. enjoys uncontested hegemony to a multipolar region. The U.S. will face more competition from China and India over access to Middle East oil.

Throughout its history, the Middle East has been the center of an imperial tug of war with major implications for the region's inhabitants. This was the case during the Cold War years. In the decade after the fall of the Soviet Union the U.S. enjoyed uncontested hegemony in a unipolar Middle East. The rise of China and India is driving the Middle East back to multipolarity. In the coming years the Middle East will turn increasingly to Asia to market its oil and gas. By 2015 it will provide 70% of Asia's oil. By far the most important growth market for countries like Iran and Saudi Arabia is China. With 1.3 billion people and an economy growing at a phenomenal rate, China is today the world's second largest oil consumer and is becoming heavily dependent on imported oil. By 2030 China is expected to import as much oil as America does today. To fuel its growing economy China is following America's footsteps, subjugating its foreign policy to its energy needs. China attempts to gain a foothold in the Middle East and build up long-term strategic links with countries with which the U.S. is at odds, like Iran, Saudi Arabia and Sudan. Though some optimists think that China's pursuit of energy could present an opportunity to enhance cooperation, integration and interdependence with the U.S., there are ample signs that China and the U.S. are already on a collision course over oil. This will have profound implications for the future and stability of the Middle East and for America's posture in the region.

America's current oil policy is inconsistent with the hallmark of the Bush Administration's foreign policy: bringing democracy and political reform to areas where democracy is in deficit.

For China the biggest prize in the Middle East is Saudi Arabia, home of a quarter of the world's reserves. Since 9/11, a deep tension in U.S.-Saudi relations has provided the Chinese with an opportunity to win the heart of the House of Saud. The Saudis fear that if their citizens again perpetrate a terror attack in the U.S., there would be no alternative for the

U.S. but to terminate its long-standing commitment to the monarchy—and perhaps even use military force against it. The Saudis realize that to forestall such a scenario they can no longer rely solely on the U.S. to defend the regime and must diversify their security portfolio. In their search for a new patron, they might find China the most fitting and willing candidate.

China has also set its sights on Iran. [In 2004] China and Iran entered a $70 billion natural gas deal that Beijing sees as critical to continued economic expansion. China has already announced that it will block any effort to impose sanctions against Iran in the UN Security Council. No doubt that as China's oil demand grows so will its involvement in Middle East politics. China is likely to provide not only diplomatic support but also weapons, including assistance in the development of WMD [weapons of mass destruction].

In sum, the prospect of a region, scarred by decades of rivalries, turning once again into an arena of competition between two or more of the major powers could well be one of the most important geo-strategic developments of the 21st-Century, with profound implications for U.S. national security.

Oil Rich, Democracy Poor

The sudden enrichment of OPEC members will undercut efforts to promote democracy and political and economic reforms in the Middle East.

It is a sad fact of life that most of the world's leading oil producing countries are either politically unstable and/or at serious odds with the U.S. With the exception of Canada and Norway, all major oil-exporting countries suffer from severe social illnesses due to their failure to absorb the shock of an oil jackpot and distribute the wealth on an equitable basis. This is not an accident. Countries rich in easily extracted and highly lucrative natural resources do not have to invest in education, productivity, or economic diversification. In addition, the government does not feel obligated to be accountable or transparent to its people and it denies them representation. They also have no imperative to educate women and grant them equal rights. While their oil wealth allows them to be the strategic pivot of world politics and economy, these "trust fund" states' record on human rights, political stability and compliance with international law is abysmal. Only three of the world's ten largest oil producers are democracies and only 9 percent of the world's proven oil reserves are in the hands of countries ranked "free" by Freedom House.

America's current oil policy is inconsistent with the hallmark of the Bush Administration's foreign policy: bringing democracy and political reform to areas where democracy is in deficit. Oil revenues help despots sustain antidemocratic social and political systems, giving them disincentives to embrace social and economic reforms. Our dependence on foreign oil often prevents the U.S. from expressing its true feelings about some of the conducts and practices of oil producing countries. Only [recently] the Bush Administration waived sanctions against Saudi Arabia, Kuwait and Ecuador, three of the word's worst offenders in human trafficking. In the case of Saudi Arabia and Kuwait the administration's explanation was that it was "in U.S. interest to continue democracy programs and security cooperation in the war on terrorism." One could only wonder if those two countries would have received the same treatment had they been major exporters of watermelons.

The Fewer Scruples, the More Oil

While in many cases the U.S. can turn a blind eye to human rights violations by major energy producers, in some cases the violations are so blunt and atrocious that a strong castigation is unavoidable. But with China joining the great oil game, such incidents result in significant weakening of U.S. geopolitical posture. In the most recent incident when the U.S. had to choose between oil and its values the cost was high: the U.S. publicly expressed dismay over the killing of hundreds of demonstrators in Uzbekistan only to be asked to remove its military forces from there within 180 days. A $600 million gas deal signed between Uzbekistan and China bolstered [Uzbek president] Islam Karimov's confidence in China's diplomatic support to the degree that he was willing to show the U.S. the door.

The Uzbek case is a harbinger of things to come. Unlike the U.S. which bars companies from doing business with some unsavory regimes China's state-owned companies turn a blind eye to the way petrodollars are used by the local governments. In the global contest for oil the U.S. loses ground as a result of its pressure for government reform. Dictators who view democracy with suspicion don't like to be pressured to reform, especially when U.S. pressure can bring an end to their regimes. They much more prefer selling their oil to countries which turn a blind eye to the way petrodollars are used and who are willing to pay top dollars for oil and not lecture to them on democracy and human rights.

The growing economic power of OPEC producers enables them to resist U.S. pressure on a variety of issues from human rights to nuclear proliferation. As the second largest oil producer and holder of 10 percent of the world's proven oil reserves Iran is fully aware of the power of its oil. Its supreme leader, Ayatollah Ali Khamenei, warned in 2002: "If the west did not receive oil, their factories would grind to a halt. This will shake the world!" The Iranians also know that oil is their insurance policy and that the best way to forestall U.S. efforts in the UN is by bedding themselves with energy hungry powers such as Japan and the two fastest-growing energy consumers—China and India. After securing the support of a third of humanity the Iranians are unfazed by the pressure coming from the U.S. and the EU. [Recently] Iran's President Mahmoud Ahmadinejad warned that Iran could wield the oil weapon if Tehran's case was sent to the Security Council for possible sanctions. . . .

Energy Myths

It is essential that we view our geopolitical situation in the context of our oil dependence and realize that it will be extremely difficult to win the war on terror and spread democracy around the world as long as we continue to send petrodollars to those who do not share our vision and values. As long as the U.S. remains dependent on oil to the degree that its does today, its dependence on the Middle East will grow. The U.S. can no longer afford to postpone urgent action to strengthen its energy security and it must begin a bold process toward reducing its demand for oil.

In order to achieve this it is important to dispel two myths:

Myth 1: The U.S. can end its dependence on the Middle East by diversifying its sources beyond the region.

While there is no alternative to dependence on Middle Eastern oil, there are clearly alternatives to oil.

Since oil is a fungible commodity [that is, oil from one place can be substituted for oil from another place], it does not matter what proportion of the oil the U.S. imports comes from the Middle East; what matters is the share of Middle East producers in overall supply. The oil market is like a huge pool: producers pour in oil while consumers draw it out. Prices and supply levels are determined in the international markets. If all we do is shuffle around our sources of oil supply, but demand for oil does not drop, the influx of petrodollars to proliferators and apologists for radical Islam as well as the vulnerability of the U.S. to international oil terrorism would remain the same even if the U.S. did not import a drop of oil from the Middle East.

Myth 2: The U.S. can drill its way out of its energy problem.

Tapping our domestic reserves which, all included, amount to less than 3% of the world's reserves, is no more than a stopgap solution. Considering America's vast long term needs our domestic reserves are a drop in the bucket. Assuming that all the oil that is claimed to be in Alaska is indeed there, the U.S.'s share of world oil would increase by less than half of a percent. No doubt unconventional petroleum sources available in the Western Hemisphere like Canadian tar sands and Venezuelan extra heavy crude could provide some relief but by no means can they significantly reduce America's dependence on the Middle East.

Alternatives to Oil

While there is no alternative to dependence on Middle Eastern oil, there are clearly alternatives to oil, particularly in the transportation sector, where two-thirds of U.S. oil is consumed.

America needs an out-of-the-barrel energy policy, one that will gradually diminish the role of oil in world politics. The U.S. should embark on an accelerated shift, enabled by modern technology, toward an economy based on indigenously produced next-generation fuels, meaning non-oil based transportation fuels such as methanol, ethanol, biodiesel, electricity and others derived from abundant domestic energy resources such as coal, biomass [plant matter], and municipal waste. In Brazil ethanol made from sugar cane accounts for at least 25% of the liquid fuel used in most cars. Many cars run on pure ethanol. As a result sugar cane ethanol comprises 40% of Brazil's fuel needs and the country is moving rapidly toward energy independence.

5

U.S. Arms Sales Undermine Stability in the Middle East

Katie Mounts and Travis Sharp

Katie Mounts is a policy associate and office manager, and Travis Sharp is the communications director and military policy analyst at the Center for Arms Control and Non-Proliferation.

The United States is the biggest seller of weapons to the Middle East. It relies on arms sales to advance its goals in the Middle East. For instance, it sells weapons to friendly regimes in order to strengthen them against America's enemy, Iran. Using arms sales in this way is dangerous, however, because friendly regimes sometimes turn hostile, and the weapons then end up in enemy hands. Thus, Osama bin Laden initially got weapons and training from the United States to fight against the Soviet Union in Afghanistan. Furthermore, U.S. arms sales are often made to undemocratic regimes, which use the weapons to maintain control over their own people. The Middle East would be safer and more democratic if the United States greatly reduced its sales of armaments to the region.

In July 2007, the United States announced the sale of $20 billion in advanced weaponry to Saudi Arabia and its neighbors of the Gulf Cooperation Council. Saudi Arabia and the United Arab Emirates are slated to receive advanced satellite-guided bomb technology known as Joint Direct Attack Munitions (JDAMs). Kuwait and the United Arab Emirates will receive, *inter alia*, [among other things] Patriot Advanced Capability-3 and -2 (PAC-3 and PAC-2) missiles.

Katie Mounts and Travis Sharp, "As Substitute For Diplomacy, $20 Billion U.S. Arms Deal Falls Short," *Center for Arms Control and Non-Proliferation*, January 14, 2008. Reproduced by permission.

Bush administration officials have indicated that the $20 billion arms deal is primarily aimed at containing Iran. Supplementary rationales for the deal include the fortification of American influence vis-à-vis peer competitors in the Middle East, future business for the United States providing spare parts, and reassurance of Gulf allies in advance of the withdrawal of U.S. combat forces from Iraq.

From 1999 to 2006, Kuwait, the United Arab Emirates, and Saudi Arabia ranked in the top five in the Middle East for the total value of their arms transfer agreements with the United States (Egypt and Israel ranked 1st and 2nd, respectively). The United Arab Emirates received $7 billion in arms transfer agreements ($892 million annual average), Saudi Arabia received $6.5 billion ($815 million annual average), and Kuwait received $3 billion ($334 million annual average) during this period in inflation-adjusted Fiscal Year 2006 dollars.

Arms Instead of Diplomacy

The United States has consistently used deadly technologies as the currency of friendship with foreign nations. From 1999 to 2006, the value of all U.S. arms transfer agreements worldwide was slightly less than the next five highest suppliers combined (Russia, France, United Kingdom, Germany, China). The United States supplied 56% of all arms transfer agreements with the Middle East during the same period. That is five times greater than Russia's proportion, the second highest supplier, and almost twenty times greater than China's proportion.

Previous experiences with Iran and Iraq illustrate that selling arms to strategic allies can backfire if the regime or relationship changes. The United States supplied Iraq with cluster bombs and chemical weapons in the 1980s, only to fight the Iraqi military in 1991 and again in 2003 and watch helplessly in the 1980s as Saddam Hussein brutally murdered thousands of Kurds [an Iraqi ethnic minority]. Iran made one-third of its defense purchases from the United States during the 1970s, but the two countries are now approaching their third decade of always chilly and sometimes hostile relations.

Instead of working with countries to improve political freedom, the $20 billion sale rewards an oppressive Saudi monarchy whose human rights record has not met expectations of improvement following the accession to the throne of King Abdullah in August 2005. Moderate Muslims throughout the world resent American involvement in the perpetuation of oppressive regimes through the sale of advanced weaponry. . . .

Guns Against Iran

Bush administration officials have clearly demonstrated that the $20 billion arms deal is primarily aimed at containing Iran. Aggressive rhetoric (including President Bush's now-infamous "World War III" remark), $60 million for democracy promotion during Fiscal Year 2008 in Iran (which has been categorically rejected by its intended Iranian recipients), financial sanctions (including the push for tougher U.N. sanctions), and the designations of the Revolutionary Guards Corps as a proliferator of weapons of mass destruction and its elite Quds force as a terrorist organization are all telltale signs that high-level U.S. policymakers are pushing back against what they see as Iranian over-encroachment.

Arms exports to the Gulf States are seen by the United States as a way to fortify American influence vis-à-vis peer competitors in the region.

A senior official involved in negotiations for the deal told the *Washington Post* on July 28, 2007, that it was "Part of a larger regional strategy. . . . We're paying attention to the needs of our allies and what everyone in the region believes is a flexing of muscles by a more aggressive Iran. One way to deal with that is to make our allies and friends strong." Undersecretary of State Nicholas Burns stated on July 30, 2007, that a primary objective of the sale is to "enable these countries to strengthen their defenses and therefore, to provide a deterrence against Iranian expansionism and Iranian aggression in the future." A few days later, Secretary of State Condoleezza Rice said the Gulf arms package would "help bolster forces of moderation and support a broader strategy to counter the negative influences of [terrorist organizations] al-Qaeda, Hezbollah, Syria and Iran."

Secretary of Defense Robert Gates told representatives at a conference in Bahrain in December 2007 that Gulf security cooperation should include "shared early warning, cooperative air and missile defense, and maritime security awareness." He spoke of regional air and missile defense systems that would provide a "regional protective defense umbrella," which one can safely assume is aimed at protecting against an attack from Iran.

While it is central to American motivations, containing Iran is not the only objective of the $20 billion arms sale. Arms exports to the Gulf States are seen by the United States as a way to fortify American influence vis-à-vis peer competitors in the region. According to this logic, U.S. arms sales dissuade the Gulf States from opting to purchase Russian or Chinese weapons, which would result in an increase in Russia and China's regional influence and a relative decrease in American influence. Spare parts and technology upgrades also ensure future business for the United States.

The United States may also be seeking to show commitment to Gulf allies in advance of a possible withdrawal of U.S. combat forces from Iraq. A senior defense official said July 27, 2007, that the $20 billion arms sale was designed to assure Middle Eastern allies that "Regardless of what happens in the near-term in Iraq that our commitment in the region remains firm, remains steadfast and that, in fact, we are looking to enhance and develop it." The deal aims to allay fears among allies that a U.S. troop withdrawal or reduction in Iraq will herald broader American disengagement from the international scene in general and the Middle East in particular. . . .

Bombs Instead of Democracy

It is important to recognize the bureaucratic logic behind the aggressive U.S. containment of Iran. Many senior members of the American defense intelligentsia cut their teeth developing ways to contain the Soviet Union's expansionist ambitions. You can't teach an old dog new tricks, as they say, and there is a real risk that U.S. policymakers are regurgitating old, comfortable theories to try to explain away new problems.

In 2003, the year of the Iraq invasion, the United States was single-handedly responsible for over half of all worldwide transfer agreements.

As was regrettably the case during the Cold War, many of the Arab regimes that the U.S. continues to prop up with massive arms sales commit gross human rights violations while stifling internal democratization. America should be working with countries like Saudi Arabia to improve political freedom and women's rights; instead, the impending sale rewards an oppressive monarchy whose human rights record has not met expectations of improvement following the accession to the throne of King Abdullah in August 2005.

Countries in the Middle East need more diplomacy and democracy, not more missiles and bombs. Although Secretary of State Condoleezza Rice previously disavowed the policy of achieving regional stability by propping up undemocratic regimes, the $20 billion dollar arms sale exhibits a disconnect between theory and practice. Moderate Muslims throughout the world resent American involvement in the perpetuation of these oppressive regimes through the sale of advanced weaponry.

Aggressively seeking to contain Shiite [an Islamic sect]-majority Iran today could lead the United States to unintentionally promote the same type of Sunni [another Islamic sect, often opposed to Shiites] extremism that gave rise to Al Qaeda. For example, many of the exact same Sunni extremists threatening the United States today, including Osama bin Laden, were funded and armed in Afghanistan by the United States to fight against invading Soviet forces in the 1980s. Vali Nasr and Ray Takeyh, two of the foremost Iran experts in the United States, make this exact argument in the January/February 2008 issue of *Foreign Affairs*:

> The last time the United States rallied the Arab world to contain Iran, in the 1980s, Americans ended up with a radicalized Sunni political culture that eventually yielded al Qaeda. The results may be as bad this time around: a containment policy will only help erect Sunni extremism as an ideological barrier to Shiite Iran, much as Saudi Arabia's rivalry with Iran in the 1980s played-out in South Asia and much as radical Salafis [Sunni Islam school of thought] mobilized to offset [Islamic militant group] Hezbollah's soaring popularity after the Israeli-Lebanese war in 2006. . . . Containing Iran today would mean promoting Sunni extremism—a self-defeating proposition for Washington.

As for the proposition that the United States must continue to sell arms to fortify American influence vis-à-vis peer competitors like Russia and China, the data shows that the United States is in no danger of losing its arms sales dominance anytime soon. From 1999 to 2006, the value of all U.S. arms transfer agreements worldwide was slightly less than the next five highest suppliers combined (Russia, France, United Kingdom, Germany, China). In 2003, the year of the Iraq invasion, the United States was single-handedly responsible for over half of all worldwide transfer agreements, more than three times the second highest supplier's proportion (Russia). In the Middle East, the United States' arms sale dominance is even more salient. The United States completed 56% of all arms transfer agreements with the Middle East from 1999 to 2006. That is five times greater than Russia's proportion, the second highest supplier, and almost twenty times greater than China's proportion, a country whose encroachment in supplying Middle East arms is cited as a justification for aggressive U.S. supply policies.

6

The United States Should Stay in Iraq Until Victory Is Won

James Phillips and Ted Galen Carpenter

James Phillips is a research fellow for Middle Eastern affairs at the Heritage Foundation, a conservative think tank in Washington, D.C. He is also on the board of editors of Middle East Quarterly.

The United States has made progress in Iraq—violence is down and radical Islam has been weakened. If the United States pulls out of Iraq now, this progress will be squandered. Al Qaeda will claim victory and be able to recruit more terrorists. Moreover, Iraq itself will become a terrorist state, exporting violence and instability throughout the Middle East.

The United States has paid a heavy price in Iraq, but it risks paying an even heavier price if it pulls the plug on a young democratic government besieged by Islamic radicals and the remnants of Saddam [Hussein]'s dictatorship. Such an act of surrender would be a strategic, geopolitical, humanitarian, and moral disaster.

Proponents of an immediate troop withdrawal underestimate the costs and risks of abdicating our security responsibilities in Iraq. Such a policy would be a huge boon for al-Qaeda in Iraq (AQI), which has been severely weakened by the American [troop] surge and the defection of many of its

James Phillips and Ted Galen Carpenter, "Online Discussion between James Philips and Ted Galen Carpenter: When Should the U.S. Withdraw From Iraq?" *Council on Foreign Relations*, February 25, 27, 29, 2008. Reproduced by permission. http://www.cfr.org/publication/15586.

Sunni [an Islamic sect] allies. [Al-Qaeda leader Osama] Bin Laden would trumpet a U.S. retreat as a tremendous victory. Al-Qaeda and its allies would benefit from an influx of new recruits, eager to share in that victory.

Without U.S. troops, Iraq likely would become a failed state, which AQI and other groups would exploit to launch attacks against Iraq's neighbors and perhaps the United States. Jordan, Kuwait, and Saudi Arabia would face the most immediate threat, but Turkey, Egypt, and Israel would also face growing threats from Iraq-based terrorists. The big winners would be Iran and Syria, the world's two leading state sponsors of terrorism, which would seek to turn Iraq into a stronghold for their terrorist surrogates, as they have done in Lebanon.

While Iraq is not Germany or Japan, neither is it Vietnam. It has much greater geopolitical importance due to its political weight in the Arab world and strategic location in the Persian Gulf, the center of gravity of world oil production. Instability in Iraq could easily spill over to disrupt oil exports from other gulf states, imposing significant long-term economic costs on oil importers. Unlike Vietnam, Iraq would export suicide bombers, not boat people. Unlike the Vietnamese communists, al-Qaeda has global ambitions, not merely regional goals.

Winning in Iraq

The surge has been a military success and has paved the way for an Iraqi political surge. In the last month [January–February 2008], Iraq's parliament has passed four laws that advance national reconciliation: de-baathification reform [removal of Saddam's Baathist Party influences], a limited amnesty for detainees, provincial powers, and a budget that gives Iraq's diverse constituencies an equitable share of oil revenues. Now that Iraq's government is making progress, it would be a tragic mistake to abandon it and risk creating a much greater humanitarian catastrophe and a failed state that would serve as a springboard for exporting Islamic revolution and terrorism. . . .

The struggle in Iraq is difficult, but winnable. With continued American support, the elected government of Iraq has a good chance to survive the disjointed insurgency, reach an accommodation with Sunni Arab moderates, and become an important ally in the war against terrorism. The U.S. cannot afford to withdraw many of its troops until the Iraqi government has adequate time to build up its own security forces. Iraq may never become a Jeffersonian democracy, but the present government with all its warts is far preferable to what is likely to emerge if the U.S. irresponsibly abandons its Iraqi allies.

[Cato Institute commentator] Ted Carpenter is overly pessimistic about the prospects for salvaging a friendly government and surprisingly optimistic about the manifold spillover effects of an American defeat. He allows that U.S. "prestige" may suffer, but glosses over the implications of a defeat for the war against al-Qaeda, efforts to contain Iran, growing Islamic radical threats in the region, the loss of Iraqi oil exports in the tight world oil market, and the humanitarian consequences for the Iraqi people. While he is concerned about giving al-Qaeda a recruiting poster, he seems remarkably unruffled by allowing it to establish a sanctuary in the heart of the Arab world in close proximity to many of the governments it seeks to overthrow.

Radical Islam Is Weakening

Iraq's dramatic drop in violence is not merely a reflection of the halt in sectarian cleansing—some of the worst violence is between rival groups of the same sect. It is due to greater realism in Iraqi politics: many Sunnis have been disabused of the notion, encouraged by Sunni Islamists and chauvinists, that they are entitled to dominate Iraq and are capable of forcibly re-imposing that domination. The backlash against AQI and other Sunni insurgent groups has been accompanied by an alienation of Shiites [an Islamic sect oppressed under Saddam] from the unruly militias that claim to defend them—about 20% of the 90,000 volunteers who have joined progovernment security forces in the last year have been Shiites.

The weakening appeal of radical Islamists on both sides is a positive development that has opened the door to greater political progress. The security gains attributable to the surge have made this possible and helped to amplify this trend. If the U.S. walks away from Iraq now, the Iraqis who have taken risks to fight our common enemies will face a devastating defeat. Abandoning Iraq would make a bad situation much worse. . . .

The U.S. has a moral obligation and a vital national interest in helping [the Iraqis] to defeat our common enemies.

The choice offered by presidential candidates is either abandoning Iraq (and dooming its people to a protracted civil war that inevitably will provide fertile ground for al-Qaeda and other hostile forces to exploit) or patiently assisting the Iraqi government to overcome formidable challenges, reaching out to Sunni Arabs, and consolidating the security gains of the surge by anchoring them in a sustainable political accommodation. The United States eventually should withdraw all troops not needed for training, logistical support, and counterterrorist operations, but it should do so at a deliberate pace calibrated according to the situation in Iraq.

Part of the War on Terror

This will be a costly enterprise. But the war in Iraq is an integral part of the war against terrorism and modern terrorists can inflict huge costs. The September 11 terrorist attacks, in addition to the deaths of almost 3,000 people, resulted in up to $639 billion of economic losses, according to a 2002 study by the New York State Senate Finance Committee. A key issue is whether a rushed withdrawal from Iraq will raise or lower the risks of future terrorist attacks.

While the Democratic presidential candidates deny that Iraq is part of the war against terrorism, al-Qaeda leaders clearly see the connection. Ayman al-Zawahiri, bin Laden's chief lieutenant, outlined plans for using Iraq as a conduit for exporting jihad to neighboring countries and attacking Israel, in an intercepted 2005 letter to Abu Musab al-Zarqawi, then the leader of al-Qaeda in Iraq. Al-Qaeda's operational commander in Afghanistan, Abu al-Layth al-Libi, declared that Iraq was "the focal point of the conflict" in a video released on April 28, 2007. The U.S. intelligence community concluded in a 2006 National Intelligence Estimate that a defeat for the United States in Iraq would be regarded as a tremendous victory for Islamic radicals and would inspire more fighters to continue the struggle elsewhere. Although the Iraq conflict may not have begun as part of the war against al-Qaeda, it is dangerously naïve to deny its relevance in that struggle.

If U.S. troops are yanked out, the hard-won progress in Iraq will rapidly evaporate, al-Qaeda will regroup and reinvigorate its efforts to provoke a civil war and transform Iraq into an incubator for jihadist terrorism. Rather than jettisoning our Iraqi allies, the U.S. has a moral obligation and a vital national interest in helping them to defeat our common enemies.

7

The United States Should Leave Iraq and Focus on Afghanistan and Pakistan

Barack Obama

Barack Obama is the forty-fourth president of the United States.

Instead of launching a war in Iraq, the United States should have concentrated on building alliances and hunting down terrorists like al Qaeda. Even though the surge in U.S. troop strength has decreased violence in Iraq, there is little political progress. Therefore, the United States needs to end its involvement in Iraq. By withdrawing carefully, the U.S. will encourage the Iraqi government to take responsibility for stability. In addition, withdrawal will free up money and troops to deal with terrorist threats in Afghanistan and Pakistan.

Imagine, for a moment, what we could have done in those days, and months, and years after 9/11.

We could have deployed the full force of American power to hunt down and destroy Osama bin Laden, al Qaeda, the Taliban, and all of the terrorists responsible for 9/11, while supporting real security in Afghanistan.

We could have secured loose nuclear materials around the world, and updated a 20th century non-proliferation framework to meet the challenges of the 21st.

We could have invested hundreds of billions of dollars in alternative sources of energy to grow our economy, save our planet, and end the tyranny of oil.

Barack Obama, "A New Strategy for a New World," *Obama for America*, July 15, 2008.

We could have strengthened old alliances, formed new partnerships, and renewed international institutions to advance peace and prosperity.

We could have called on a new generation to step into the strong currents of history, and to serve their country as troops and teachers, Peace Corps volunteers and police officers.

We could have secured our homeland—investing in sophisticated new protection for our ports, our trains and our power plants.

We could have rebuilt our roads and bridges, laid down new rail and broadband and electricity systems, and made college affordable for every American to strengthen our ability to compete.

We could have done that.

Iraq War a Distraction

Instead, we have lost thousands of American lives, spent nearly a trillion dollars, alienated allies and neglected emerging threats—all in the cause of fighting a war for well over five years in a country that had absolutely nothing to do with the 9/11 attacks.

Our men and women in uniform have accomplished every mission we have given them. What's missing in our debate about Iraq—what has been missing since before the war began—is a discussion of the strategic consequences of Iraq and its dominance of our foreign policy. This war distracts us from every threat that we face and so many opportunities we could seize. This war diminishes our security, our standing in the world, our military, our economy, and the resources that we need to confront the challenges of the 21st century. By any measure, our single-minded and open-ended focus on Iraq is not a sound strategy for keeping America safe.

I [intend as] President of the United States to lead this country in a new direction—to seize this moment's promise. Instead of being distracted from the most pressing threats that we face, I want to overcome them. Instead of pushing the entire burden of our foreign policy on to the brave men and women of our military, I want to use all elements of American power to keep us safe, and prosperous, and free. Instead of alienating ourselves from the world, I want America—once again—to lead.

As President, I will pursue a tough, smart and principled national security strategy—one that recognizes that we have interests not just in Baghdad [Iraq] but in Kandahar [Afghanistan] and Karachi [Pakistan], in Tokyo and London, in Beijing and Berlin. I will focus this strategy on five goals essential to making America safer: ending the war in Iraq responsibly: finishing the fight against al Qaeda and the Taliban; securing all nuclear weapons and materials from terrorists and rogue states; achieving true energy security; and rebuilding our alliances to meet the challenges of the 21st century. . . .

Invading Iraq Was Wrong

I opposed going to war in Iraq; . . . I warned that the invasion of a country posing no imminent threat would fan the flames of extremism, and distract us from the fight against al Qaeda and the Taliban. . . .

Now, all of us recognize that we must do more than look back—we must make a judgment about how to move forward. What is needed? What can best be done? What must be done? . . . I want to focus on a new strategy for Iraq and the wider world.

In the 18 months since the surge [in Iraq] began, the situation in Afghanistan has deteriorated.

It has been 18 months since President Bush announced the surge [an increase in U.S. troop levels]. As I have said many times, our troops have performed brilliantly in lowering the level of violence. General David Petraeus has used new tactics to protect the Iraqi population. We have talked directly to Sunni [an Islamic sect] tribes that used to be hostile to America, and supported their fight against al Qaeda. Shiite [an Islamic sect, often opposed to Sunnis] militias have generally respected a cease-fire. Those are the facts, and all Americans welcome them.

Current Strategy Not Working

[My opponents have] argued that the gains of the surge mean that I should change my commitment to end the war. But this argument misconstrues what is necessary to succeed in Iraq, and stubbornly ignores the facts of the broader strategic picture that we face.

In the 18 months since the surge began, the strain on our military has increased, our troops and their families have borne an enormous burden, and American taxpayers have spent another $200 billion in Iraq. That's over $10 billion each month. That is a consequence of our current strategy.

In the 18 months since the surge began, the situation in Afghanistan has deteriorated. June [2008] was our highest casualty month of the war. The Taliban has been on the offensive, even launching a brazen attack on one of our bases. Al Qaeda has a growing sanctuary in Pakistan. That is a consequence of our current strategy.

In the 18 months since the surge began, as I warned at the outset—Iraq's leaders have not made the political progress that was the purpose of the surge. They have not invested tens of billions of dollars in oil revenues to rebuild their country. They have not resolved their differences or shaped a new political compact.

End the War

That's why I strongly stand by my plan to end this war. Now [Iraqi] Prime Minister Maliki's call for a timetable for the removal of U.S. forces presents a real opportunity. It comes at a time when the American general in charge of training Iraq's Security Forces has testified that Iraq's Army and Police will be ready to assume responsibility for Iraq's security in 2009. Now is the time for a responsible redeployment of our combat troops that pushes Iraq's leaders toward a political solution, rebuilds our military, and refocuses on Afghanistan and our broader security interests.

We must be as careful getting out of Iraq as we were careless getting in.

[The Republicans] don't have a strategy for success in Iraq—they have a strategy for staying in Iraq. They said we couldn't leave when violence was up, they say we can't leave when violence is down. They refuse to press the Iraqis to make tough choices, and they label any timetable to redeploy our troops "surrender," even though we would be turning Iraq over to a sovereign Iraqi government—not to a terrorist enemy. Theirs is an endless focus on tactics inside Iraq, with no consideration of our strategy to face threats beyond Iraq's borders.

At some point, a judgment must be made. Iraq is not going to be a perfect place, and we don't have unlimited resources to try to make it one. We are not going to kill every al Qaeda sympathizer, eliminate every trace of Iranian influence, or stand up a flawless democracy before we leave—General Petraeus and [U.S.] Ambassador [to Iraq] Ryan Crocker acknowledged this to me when they testified [before Congress in April 2008]. That is why the accusation of surrender is false rhetoric used to justify a failed policy. In fact, true success in Iraq—victory in Iraq—will not take place in a surrender ceremony where an enemy lays down their arms. True success will take place when we leave Iraq to a government that is taking responsibility for its future—a government that prevents sectarian conflict, and ensures that the al Qaeda threat which has been beaten back by our troops does not reemerge. That is an achievable goal if we pursue a comprehensive plan to press the Iraqis to stand up.

A Careful Withdrawal

To achieve that success, I will give our military a new mission: ... ending this war. Let me be clear: we must be as careful getting out of Iraq as we were careless getting in. We can safely redeploy our combat brigades at a pace that would remove them in 16 months. That would be the summer of 2010—one year after Iraqi Security Forces will be prepared to stand up; two years from now, and more than seven years after the war began. After this redeployment, we'll keep a residual force to perform specific missions in Iraq: targeting any remnants of al Qaeda; protecting our service members and diplomats; and training and supporting Iraq's Security Forces, so long as the Iraqis make political progress.

We will make tactical adjustments as we implement this strategy—that is what any responsible Commander-in-Chief must do. As I have consistently said, I will consult with commanders on the ground and the Iraqi government. We will redeploy from secure areas first and volatile areas later. We will commit $2 billion to a meaningful international effort to support the more than 4 million displaced Iraqis. We will forge a new coalition to support Iraq's future—one that includes all of Iraq's neighbors, and also the United Nations, the World Bank, and the European Union—because we all have a stake in stability. And we will make it clear that the United States seeks no permanent bases in Iraq.

This is the future that Iraqis want. This is the future that the American people want. And this is what our common interests demand. Both America and Iraq will be more secure when the terrorist in Anbar [province in Iraq] is taken out by the Iraqi Army, and the criminal in Baghdad fears Iraqi Police, not just coalition forces. Both America and Iraq will succeed when every Arab government has an embassy open in Baghdad, and the child in Basra [Iraq] benefits from services provided by Iraqi dinars [Iraqi currency], not American tax dollars.

And this is the future we need for our military. We cannot tolerate this strain on our forces to fight a war that hasn't made us safer. I will restore our strength by ending this war, completing the increase of our ground forces by 65,000 soldiers and 27,000 marines, and investing in the capabilities we need to defeat conventional foes and meet the unconventional challenges of our time.

So let's be clear. . . . I want Iraqis to take responsibility for their own future, and to reach the political accommodation necessary for long-term stability. That's victory. That's success. That's what's best for Iraq, that's what's best for America, and that's why I will end this war as President.

War in Afghanistan

In fact . . . the central front in the war on terror is not Iraq, and it never was. That's why the second goal of my new strategy will be taking the fight to al Qaeda in Afghanistan and Pakistan.

It is unacceptable that almost seven years after nearly 3,000 Americans were killed on our soil, the terrorists who attacked us on 9/11 are still at large. Osama bin Laden and Ayman al-Zawahari are recording messages to their followers and plotting more terror. The Taliban controls parts of Afghanistan. Al Qaeda has an expanding base in Pakistan that is probably no farther from their old Afghan sanctuary than a train ride from Washington to Philadelphia. If another attack on our homeland comes, it will likely come from the same region where 9/11 was planned. And yet today, we have five times more troops in Iraq than Afghanistan. . . .

Our troops and our NATO allies are performing heroically in Afghanistan, but I have argued for years that we lack the resources to finish the job because of our commitment to Iraq. That's what the Chairman of the Joint Chiefs of Staff said. And that's why, as President, I will make the fight against al Qaeda and the Taliban the top priority that it should be. This is a war that we have to win.

We need a stronger and sustained partnership between Afghanistan, Pakistan and NATO to secure the border, to take out terrorist camps, and to crack down on cross-border insurgents.

I will send at least two additional combat brigades to Afghanistan, and use this commitment to seek greater contributions—with fewer restrictions—from NATO allies. I will focus on training Afghan security forces and supporting an Afghan judiciary, with more resources and incentives for American officers who perform these missions. Just as we succeeded in the Cold War by supporting allies who could sustain their own security, we must realize that the 21st century's frontlines are not only on the field of battle—they are found in the training exercise near Kabul, in the police station in Kandahar, and in the rule of law in Herat.

Moreover, lasting security will only come if we heed [the creator of the post–World War II reconstruction plan, George] Marshall's lesson, and help Afghans grow their economy from the bottom up. That's why I've proposed an additional $1 billion in non-military assistance each year, with meaningful safeguards to prevent corruption and to make sure investments are made—not just in Kabul—but out in Afghanistan's provinces. As a part of this program, we'll invest in alternative livelihoods to poppy-growing for Afghan farmers, just as we crack down on heroin trafficking. We cannot lose Afghanistan to a future of narco-terrorism. The Afghan people must know that our commitment to their future is enduring, because the security of Afghanistan and the United States is shared.

The greatest threat to that security lies in the tribal regions of Pakistan, where terrorists train and insurgents strike into Afghanistan. We cannot tolerate a terrorist sanctuary, and as President, I won't. We need a stronger and sustained partnership between Afghanistan, Pakistan and NATO to secure the border, to take out terrorist camps, and to crack down on cross-border insurgents. We need more troops, more helicopters, more satellites, more Predator drones in the Afghan border region. And we must make it clear that if Pakistan cannot or will not act, we will take out high-level terrorist targets like bin Laden if we have them in our sights.

8

The United States Should Highlight al Qaeda's Atrocities in the Middle East

Gary Anderson

Gary Anderson led a study of al Qaeda from 2003 to 2005 and has served as an adviser to the Defense Department on counterinsurgency operations. He teaches at the Elliot School of International Affairs at George Washington University.

The terrorist group al Qaeda is weakening. In places where al Qaeda has been established for a long time, such as Iraq and Afghanistan, support for it falls. This is because al Qaeda's agents are foreigners in most of the places they operate and because their methods are brutal. To win over people in the Middle East, the United States should spend less time trying to promote our own values, which are not popular, and more time highlighting the atrocities al Qaeda commits against Muslims.

The conventional wisdom is that al-Qaeda is making a comeback from its rout in Afghanistan. Many point to its success in killing [Pakistani leader] Benazir Bhutto in Pakistan and to its support of Islamic insurgents there as evidence. Not so. Al-Qaeda is waning. Its decline has less to do with our success than with the institutional limitations of the al-Qaeda organization. Simply stated, to know al-Qaeda closely is not to love it.

Everyplace where al-Qaeda has gained some measure of control over a civilian population, it has quickly worn out its

Gary Anderson, "Why Al-Qaeda Is Losing," washingtonpost.com, January 13, 2008. Reproduced by permission.

welcome. This happened in Kabul [Afghanistan] and in Anbar province in western Iraq. It may well happen in Pakistan as a reaction to the killing of Bhutto.

No one likes to be brutalized and dominated by foreigners. The weakness of al-Qaeda is that everywhere it goes its people are strangers. This is no way to build a worldwide caliphate.

Focus on Them, Not Us

We may not be loved in Iraq and Afghanistan, but compared with the deliberately brutal methods of bin Laden's associates we become a palatable alternative. This is particularly true because, like visiting grandchildren, we will eventually go home.

Bhutto once responded to a friend who was concerned about her safety by saying, "Muslims don't kill women." She was only partly right; real Muslims don't do that, but al-Qaeda does. Its members have killed more Muslim civilians than have misdirected coalition airstrikes in Iraq and Afghanistan combined. The difference is that the Americans and their allies regret and investigate such incidents: al-Qaeda plans and celebrates them.

I would spend my dollars on collecting photos of the Muslim innocents al-Qaeda has killed and putting below them quotations from the Koran decrying such practices.

Why, then, are we supposedly losing the information war in the Muslim world, and why has there not been more of an outcry among Muslims over this slaughter of innocents? A big part of the reason is that we spend too much time wanting to be liked rather than turning Muslim anger on our enemies.

We preach some values that are viewed as alien and threatening to the traditional order of things. Our popular culture is seen as decadent at best and downright threatening at worst in traditional cultures. Our message isn't selling. We can't change what we are, nor would we want to. No matter how much the government may disapprove, the government's official propaganda will be overwhelmed by the deluge, both positive and negative, from the popular media. We need to accept this fact and move on, rather than waste more millions on strategic communications "charm campaigns."

Help al-Qaeda Destroy Itself

What we can do is to expose our Islamic extremist enemies for what they are. The people of Afghanistan and Anbar found this out the hard way and threw the rascals out. But when al-Qaeda kills scores of innocents, we report it as a statistic without context. We may see weeping relatives and bloodstained bodies from a distance, on video or in photographs, but they are depersonalized, and people quickly become desensitized to anonymous images. Ironically, [Soviet dictator Joseph] Stalin was right: One death is a tragedy; millions are a statistic. We need to help Muslims understand how these people really treat other Muslims.

The original Islamic movement spread its doctrine by a combination of military action and compassion. Charity was a key tenet. This is largely why [militant Islamist groups] Hamas and Hezbollah gain a degree of popular support in the areas they control. That ingredient is missing in the al-Qaeda/ Taliban approach to the world. To them, winning hearts and minds means, "Agree with us or else." That is largely the reason that the U.S. government dropped its early "for us or against us" approach. It has taken us some time, but we seem to be recovering from that approach.

If I were directing the U.S. strategic information campaign, I would spend my dollars on collecting photos of the Muslim innocents al-Qaeda has killed and putting below them quotations from the Koran decrying such practices. These advertisements would appear in every newspaper and TV station in the Muslim world where I could buy print space or air time.

We may not be losing the war on terrorism, but we are not doing all that we can to win it.

9

The United States Should Bomb Iran

Joshua Muravchik

Joshua Muravchik is a scholar at the American Enterprise Institute for Public Policy Research. He is the author of Exporting Democracy: Fulfilling America's Destiny *(1991) and an editorial board member of the journal* World Affairs.

Despite sanctions and diplomacy, Iran continues its efforts to develop nuclear weapons. A nuclear Iran would be extremely dangerous to the United States. Iran has ties with terrorists and might supply them with nuclear materials. In addition, Iran has vowed to destroy Israel and might well use nuclear weapons to do so. Finally, nuclear weapons would allow Iran to challenge the United States in the Middle East, leading to a terrible global struggle. To prevent these dangers, the United States should destroy Iranian nuclear facilities with targeted bombs.

We must bomb Iran.

It has been four years since that country's secret nuclear program was brought to light [in 2002], and the path of diplomacy and sanctions has led nowhere.

First, we agreed to our allies' requests that we offer Tehran a string of concessions, which it spurned. Then, Britain, France and Germany wanted to impose a batch of extremely weak sanctions. For instance, Iranians known to be involved in

Joshua Muravchik, "Bomb Iran: Diplomacy is doing nothing to stop the Iranian nuclear threat; a show of force is the only answer," *Los Angeles Times*, November 19, 2006. Reproduced by permission.

nuclear activities would have been barred from foreign travel—except for humanitarian or religious reasons—and outside countries would have been required to refrain from aiding some, but not all, Iranian nuclear projects.

But even this was too much for the U.N. Security Council. Russia promptly announced that these sanctions were much too strong. "We cannot support measures ... aimed at isolating Iran," declared Foreign Minister Sergei V. Lavrov.

Sanctions Will Not Work

It is now clear that neither Moscow nor Beijing will ever agree to tough sanctions. What's more, even if they were to do so, it would not stop Iran, which is a country on a mission. As President Mahmoud Ahmadinejad put it: "Thanks to the blood of the martyrs, a new Islamic revolution has arisen. . . . The era of oppression, hegemonic regimes and tyranny and injustice has reached its end. . . . The wave of the Islamic revolution will soon reach the entire world." There is simply no possibility that Iran's clerical rulers will trade this ecstatic vision for a mess of Western pottage[1] in the form of economic bribes or penalties.

We cannot live safely with a nuclear-armed Iran.

So if sanctions won't work, what's left? The overthrow of the current Iranian regime might offer a silver bullet, but with hard-liners firmly in the saddle in Tehran, any such prospect seems even more remote today than it did a decade ago, when students were demonstrating and reformers were ascendant. Meanwhile, the completion of Iran's bomb grows nearer every day.

Our options therefore are narrowed to two: We can prepare to live with a nuclear-armed Iran, or we can use force to

---

1. A biblical reference to Genesis 25:29–34, where the patriarch Isaac's eldest son, Esau, trades his inheritance to his younger brother, Jacob, for a bowl of stew, translated in the King James Bible as a "mess of pottage."

prevent it. Former ABC newsman Ted Koppel argues for the former, saying that "if Iran is bound and determined to have nuclear weapons, let it." We should rely, he says, on the threat of retaliation to keep Iran from using its bomb. Similarly, *Newsweek International* editor Fareed Zakaria points out that we have succeeded in deterring other hostile nuclear states, such as the Soviet Union and China.

And in [the *L.A. Times*] William Langewiesche summed up the what-me-worry? attitude when he wrote that "the spread of nuclear weapons is, and always has been, inevitable," and that the important thing is "learning how to live with it after it occurs."

Iran Would Use Nukes

But that's whistling past the graveyard [so as to appear un-afraid]. The reality is that we cannot live safely with a nuclear-armed Iran. One reason is terrorism, of which Iran has long been the world's premier state sponsor, through [militant Islamic] groups such as Hamas and Hezbollah. Now, according to a report in London's *Daily Telegraph*, Iran is trying to take over Al Qaeda by positioning its own man, Saif Adel, to become the successor to the ailing Osama bin Laden. How could we possibly trust Iran not to slip nuclear material to terrorists?

Koppel says that we could prevent this by issuing a blanket warning that if a nuclear device is detonated anywhere in the United States, we will assume Iran is responsible. But would any U.S. president really order a retaliatory nuclear strike based on an assumption?

Another reason is that an Iranian bomb would constitute a dire threat to Israel's 6 million-plus citizens. Sure, Israel could strike back, but Hashemi Rafsanjani, the former president who was Ahmadinejad's "moderate" electoral opponent, once pointed out smugly that "the use of an atomic bomb against Israel would totally destroy Israel, while [the same] against the Islamic world would only cause damage. Such a scenario is not inconceivable." If that is the voice of pragmatism in Iran, would you trust deterrence against the messianic Ahmadinejad?

Even if Iran did not drop a bomb on Israel or hand one to terrorists, its mere possession of such a device would have devastating consequences. Coming on top of North Korea's nuclear test, it would spell *finis* [the end] to the entire nonproliferation system.

Iran Would Be Too Powerful

And then there is a consequence that seems to have been thought about much less but could be the most harmful of all: Tehran could achieve its goal of regional supremacy. Jordan's King Abdullah II, for instance, has warned of an emerging Shiite "crescent." But Abdullah's comment understates the danger. If Iran's reach were limited to Shiites [an Islamic sect dominant in Iran], it would be constrained by their minority status in the Muslim world as well as by the divisions between Persians [ethnic group dominant in Iran] and Arabs.

But such ethnic-based analysis fails to take into account Iran's charisma as the archenemy of the United States and Israel and the leverage it achieves as the patron of radicals and rejectionists. Given that, the old assumptions about Shiites and Sunnis [another Islamic sect, often opposed to Shiites] may not hold any longer. Iran's closest ally today is Syria, which is mostly Sunni. The link between Tehran and Damascus [Syria's capital] is ideological, not theological. Similarly, Iran supports the Palestinian groups Islamic Jihad and Hamas, which are overwhelmingly Sunni (and as a result, Iran has grown popular in the eyes of Palestinians).

During the Lebanon war [in 2006], we saw how readily Muslims closed ranks across the Sunni-Shiite divide against a common foe (even as the two groups continued killing each other in Iraq). In Sunni Egypt, newborns were named "Hezbollah" after the Lebanese Shiite organization and "Nasrallah" after its leader. As Muslim scholar Vail Nasr put it: "A flurry of anti-Hezbollah [i.e., anti-Shiite] *fatwas* [decrees] by radical Sunni clerics have not diverted the admiring gaze of Arabs everywhere toward Hezbollah."

In short, Tehran can build influence on a mix of ethnicity and ideology, underwritten by the region's largest economy. Nuclear weapons would bring regional hegemony within its reach by intimidating neighbors and rivals and stirring the admiration of many other Muslims.

A New Cold War

This would thrust us into a new global struggle akin to the one we waged so painfully with the Soviet Union for 40-odd years. It would be the "clash of civilizations" that has been so much talked about but so little defined.

Iran might seem little match for the United States, but that is not how Ahmadinejad sees it. He and his fellow jihadists believe that the Muslim world has already defeated one infidel superpower (the Soviet Union) and will in time defeat the other.

Wouldn't . . . a U.S. air attack on Iran inflame global anti-Americanism?. . . Yes, probably. That is the price we would pay. But the alternative is worse.

Russia was poor and weak in 1917 when [Vladimir] Lenin took power, as was Germany in 1933 when [Adolf] Hitler came in. Neither, in the end, was able to defeat the United States, but each of them unleashed unimaginable suffering before they succumbed. And despite its weakness, Iran commands an asset that neither of them had: a natural advantage in appealing to the world's billion-plus Muslims.

If Tehran establishes dominance in the region, then the battlefield might move to Southeast Asia or Africa or even parts of Europe, as the mullahs [Iranian religious leaders] would try to extend their sway over other Muslim peoples. In the end, we would no doubt win, but how long this contest might last and what toll it might take are anyone's guess.

Strike First

The only way to forestall these frightening developments is by the use of force. Not by invading Iran as we did Iraq, but by an air campaign against Tehran's nuclear facilities. We have considerable information about these facilities; by some estimates they comprise about 1,500 targets. If we hit a large fraction of them in a bombing campaign that might last from a few days to a couple of weeks, we would inflict severe damage. This would not end Iran's weapons program, but it would certainly delay it. . . . In time, if Tehran persisted, we might have to do it again.

Can President [George W.] Bush take such action after being humiliated in the [2006] congressional elections and with the Iraq war having grown so unpopular? Bush has said that history's judgment on his conduct of the war against terror is more important than the polls. If Ahmadinejad gets his finger on a nuclear trigger, everything Bush has done will be rendered hollow. We will be a lot less safe than we were when Bush took office.

Finally, wouldn't such a U.S. air attack on Iran inflame global anti-Americanism? Wouldn't Iran retaliate in Iraq or by terrorism? Yes, probably. That is the price we would pay. But the alternative is worse.

After the Bolshevik takeover of Russia in 1917, a single member of Britain's Cabinet, Winston Churchill, appealed for robust military intervention to crush the new regime. His colleagues weighed the costs—the loss of soldiers, international derision, revenge by Lenin—and rejected the idea.

The costs were avoided, and instead the world was subjected to the greatest man-made calamities ever. Communism itself was to claim perhaps 100 million lives, and it also gave rise to fascism and Nazism, leading to World War II. Ahmadinejad wants to be the new Lenin. Force is the only thing that can stop him.

10

The United States Should Negotiate with Iran

Christopher Hitchens

Christopher Hitchens is an author, journalist, and critic. His 2003 book The Long Short War: The Postponed Liberation of Iraq *is a collection of essays supporting the American invasion of Iraq.*

Bombing Iran to destroy its nuclear weapons program probably will not work. Luckily, the Iranian government is not insane, as Saddam Hussein was. Moreover, the Iranian people favor re-opening diplomatic relations with the United States. In light of this, the United States should end sanctions against Iran and normalize diplomatic relations. This is the best way to stabilize the region and to win nuclear concessions from Iran.

The most touching remark I heard during my time in Iran [in 2005] was from a woman in the wonderfully beautiful city of Isfahan. (It is just outside this cultural treasure house that the *mullahs* [Iranian religious/political leaders] have chosen to place one of their mountain-dugout nuclear sites.) In the family home where I was staying, contempt and hatred for theocracy was a given, but this was a family friend, moreover draped in a deep black chador [full body cloak worn by some Muslim women] who stayed on the edge of the conversation. Finally she broke in to ask shyly, in faultless English, "Would it be possible for the Americans to invade just for a few days, get rid of the mullahs and the weapons, and then leave?"

Christopher Hitchens, "Survey Says: Let the Exchange of Trade and Ideas with Iran Begin," slate.com, March 6, 2006. Reproduced by permission.

My heart went out to her. And I would guess, from travel-
ing around several Iranian cities, that there are very many Iranians who are wishful along just those lines. They dream of
some magic trick that would just make the bearded ones go
away, restore Iran to the international community, and yet not
compromise its cherished national pride and independence.
My guess would also be that, of the millions who want the
mullahs gone, very few would support an outside military intervention if it actually occurred. In other words, the most
precious asset that the United States has in the current crisis
[over Iran's nuclear program]—a large pro-American public
opinion in Iran—is apparently not of much use to it in decid-
ing what to do about the weapons program.

All the war games and simulations that I have seen have
concluded that it isn't possible to disarm Iran by airstrikes.
Learning perhaps from what happened to [Iraqi dictator] Saddam [Hussein]'s nuclear plant at Osirak the authorities have
dispersed the program widely and put a lot of it underground.
Nor can the Israelis be expected to do much by proxy: They
would have to fly over Iraq this time, and it would be even
more obvious than usual that they were acting as an American surrogate. Professor Edward Luttwak claims, in the *Wall
Street Journal*, that selective strikes could still retard or de-
grade the program, but this, if true, would only restate the
problem in a different form.

Diplomacy Is the Best Option

This means that our options are down to three: reliance on
the United Nations/European Union bargaining table, a "de-
capitating" military strike, or Nixon goes to China.[1] The first
being demonstrably useless and somewhat humiliating, and
the second being possibly futile as well as hazardous, it might
be worth giving some thought to the third of these. Assume

1. U.S. President Richard Nixon visited China in 1972 in an effort to lower tensions between the two nations.

that the Iranians are within measurable distance of nuclear status. Appearances sometimes to the contrary, they are not mad—or not clinically insane in the way that Saddam Hussein was and [North Korean leader] Kim Jong-il is. The recent fuss about the obliteration of Israel is largely bullshit: [former Iranian religious/political leader] Ayatollah Khomeini's call for this has been intoned pedantically and routinely ever since he first uttered it, and it only got attention [recently] because of the new phenomenon of Mahmoud Ahmadinejad, the scrofulous [corrupt] engineer who acts the part of civilian president for his clerical bosses. These people (who once bought weapons from Israel via [U.S. operative] Oliver North in order to fight Saddam Hussein) are cynical and corrupt. They know as well as you do what would happen if they tried to nuke Israel or the United States. They want the bomb as insurance against invasion and as a weapon of strategic ambiguity to shore up their position in the region.

In Iran . . . surveys have shown that a huge majority converges on one point: that it is time to resume diplomatic relations with the United States.

They Want to Talk to Us

But they have a crucial vulnerability on the inside. The overwhelmingly young population—an ironic result of the mullahs' attempt to increase the birth rate after the calamitous war with Iraq—is fed up with medieval rule. Unlike the hermetic societies of [Saddam's] Baathist Iraq and North Korea, Iran has been forced to permit a lot of latitude to its citizens. A huge number of them have relatives in the West, access to satellite dishes and cell phones, and regular contact with neighboring societies. They are appalled at the way that Turkey, for example, has evolved into a near-European state while Iran is still stuck in enforced backwardness and stagnation, competing only in the rug and pistachio markets. Opinion polling is a new science in Iran, but several believable surveys have shown that a huge majority converges on one point: that it is time to resume diplomatic relations with the United States. (The vast American Embassy compound, which I visited, is for now a stupid museum of propaganda. But when one mullah recently asked if he could have a piece of the extensive grounds for a religious school, he was told by the authorities that the place must be kept intact.)

Happy Ending

So, picture if you will the landing of Air Force One at Imam Khomeini International Airport. The president emerges, reclaims the U.S. Embassy in return for an equivalent in Washington and the un-freezing of Iran's financial assets, and announces that sanctions have been a waste of time and have mainly hurt Iranian civilians. (He need not add that they have also given some clerics monopoly positions in various black markets; the populace already knows this.) A new era is possible, he goes on to say. America and the Shiite [Islamic sect dominant in Iran] world have a common enemy in [terrorist group] al-Qaida, just as they had in [former Muslim-persecuting president of Serbia] Slobodan Milosevic, the Taliban, and the Iraqi Baathists. America is home to a large and talented Iranian community. Let the exchange of trade and people and ideas begin! There might perhaps even be a ticklish-to-write paragraph, saying that America is not proud of everything it is has done in the past—most notably Jimmy Carter's criminal decision to permit Saddam to invade Iran.

The aging mullahs might claim this as a capitulation, which would be hard to bear. But how right would they be? The pressure for a new constitution and genuine elections is already building. Within less than a decade, we might be negotiating with a whole new generation of Iranians. Iran would have less incentive to disrupt progress in Iraq (and we should not forget that it has been generally not unhelpful in

Afghanistan). Eventually, Iran might have a domestic nuclear program (to which it is fully entitled and which would decrease its oil-dependency) and be ready to sign a nonproliferation agreement with enforceable and verifiable provisions. American technical help would be available for this, since it was we who (in a wonderful moment of [Henry] Kissingerian "realism") helped them build the Bushehr reactor in the first place.

Just a thought.

The United States Cannot Negotiate with Its Middle East Enemies

Orson Scott Card

Orson Scott Card is an award-winning author, known especially for his works of science fiction. His political column, called War Watch, Civilization Watch, or World Watch, appears weekly in the Greensboro, North Carolina–based Rhinoceros Times.

The enemies of the United States in the Middle East are fundamentally opposed to Western civilization. They are also liars who make promises only to break them. Therefore, the United States cannot negotiate with them. In fact, any negotiation is appeasement that legitimizes terrorists. When the Democrats promise to negotiate with terrorists, therefore, they are essentially promising to surrender. This undermines the war effort.

President [George W.] Bush went to Israel to affirm America's ironclad support of Israel's survival as a nation. While there are Americans who don't agree with it, this has been the policy of the United States from the foundation of Israel on. President Bush didn't invent the policy, but he affirms it more vigorously and intelligently than most Presidents have done.

President Bush said, "Some seem to believe that we should negotiate with the terrorists and radicals, as if some ingenious argument will persuade them they have been wrong all along."

Orson Scott Card, "What Obama Should Have Said," *World Watch*, May 18, 2008. Reproduced by permission of the author.

Not Misunderstanding, But Hatred

Thus he stated, quite clearly, how delusional are those who think that what we have in our war with radical Islam is a "failure to communicate." There is no failure: communication has been crystal clear. Our enemies have announced their firm intention to destroy our civilization, to kill all the Jews, and to kill any Muslim who doesn't go along with their program. Iran has announced its intention, if they get nuclear missiles, to obliterate [Israel's capital] Tel Aviv. Al Qaeda has declared its intention to destroy the West.

We are not misunderstanding their intentions—they have acted exactly according to these stated goals whenever they have had the power to do so.

There is nothing we can do, short of killing them or surrendering to them, that will stop them from acting as they have been acting for decades—murderously and relentlessly. There is certainly nothing we can *say*.

There are no "root causes" we can address. Al Qaeda and Iran keep changing their statements of what we have done that provokes them. We withdrew our forces from Saudi Arabia—and Al Qaeda no longer used that as their excuse for attacking us. But they kept on attacking. The excuse was the illusion—the implacable hatred was the reality.

There is no negotiation with people who have decided that everything we are and hope for and believe in must be torn down and destroyed.

Nor have they misunderstood *us*. Those who hate us are among the best-educated people in the Muslim world. The more they know us, the more they hate and fear our civilization's influence on the Muslim world. They know that radical Islam is even less well-suited to deal with modern science and technology than fundamentalist Christianity, which has made its accommodations. To match the technological and scientific superiority of the West, they have to educate their children in something other than the Quran. Therefore they want to tear down the West and make sure *everybody's* children learn nothing but the Quran. In equal ignorance, the advantage of the West would disappear.

Terrorists Are Liars

Furthermore, in the cases where we *have* negotiated with terrorists, they have almost never kept their word. When Ronald Reagan stupidly negotiated with Iran to buy, with American weapons, the freedom of hostages held in Lebanon by [militant Islamist group] Hezbollah, our hostages *were* released (except those that had already been murdered)—but they simply took more hostages. They finally stopped, not because of negotiations, but because the taking of hostages was no longer accomplishing what they wanted.

As for the Palestinians, they have never kept *any* agreement. Israel makes concessions; the Palestinians make promises. The Palestinians break the promises; Israel refuses to make any more concessions; and then the Palestinians scream that it's *Israel* that is not keeping the treaty. The Palestinians murder Israeli schoolchildren, and when Israel strikes back against terrorists, the Palestinians scream about *Israeli* aggression.

In short, there is no negotiation with people who have decided that everything we are and hope for and believe in must be torn down and destroyed. And it is amazing to me that the people *most* determined to rely on negotiations with these terrorists are precisely the people whose purported values are the first ones that these terrorists would destroy, if they were ever given the chance to decide how the West should live.

No Appeasement

I'm glad [Bush] was willing to name these "negotiators" for what they are. Here's what he said: "We have heard this foolish delusion before. As Nazi tanks crossed into Poland in 1939, an American senator declared: 'Lord, if I could only have talked to Hitler, all this might have been avoided.' We have an obligation to call this what it is: the false comfort of appeasement, which has been repeatedly discredited by history."

In Israel, where the consequences of appeasement are well-remembered, these remarks were met with a standing ovation.

Whom was Bush talking about? Obviously, [former president] Jimmy Carter, who had just gotten through talking to the leaders of terrorist groups. And he was talking about *all* the people who are so foolish they think that our campaign in Iraq somehow *provoked* the terrorists—even though every group of terrorists opposing us there was *already killing Americans* and Israelis prior to the beginning of our campaign in Iraq! *All* the people who think that if you just sit down and talk with Iran, with Hezbollah, with [Palestinian militant group] Hamas, with Al Qaeda, we can iron out our "misunderstandings." . . .

Here's what [Barack Obama] *should* have said [in his criticism of Bush's war on terror strategy]: "I applaud President Bush for opposing any attempt at appeasement of terrorists. I agree with him completely that those who negotiate from weakness will accomplish nothing. Fortunately, when I am President I will talk to them from a position of strength, demanding that they comply with the rules of civilized behavior and put an end to terrorism. There is a middle way between blind war and mindless appeasement—it is negotiation with a credible threat of force. What Republican President Theodore Roosevelt said: Speak softly and carry a big stick. Appeasers have no stick. President Bush has nothing *but* the stick."

Now, I personally think President Bush has acted more or less correctly in his dealings with terrorists and terrorist nations. But I was writing Obama's ideal campaign response. If he'd been smart, he'd have said, "President Bush is obviously not talking about me, because I have never called for appeasement."

Instead, he made President Bush's point *for* him by agreeing that President Bush had just described Obama's program.

Criticizing the President Helps Terrorists

Other clowns have chimed in. [Senator] Joe Biden proved once again how glad we all should be that he was never made president, as he called President Bush an "appeaser" for negotiating with North Korea. As if Biden had never heard of China. The fact is that you don't mess with North Korea unless you want war with China, so it is not appeasement, it is realpolitik [policy based on practical considerations]. President Bush treads softly with North Korea.

(Also, North Korea's people are starving, and it is only a matter of time before either China, the North Korean military, or a desperate popular uprising brings down the present insane, evil North Korean regime.)

What's particularly sad about Obama's response is that it is so hypocritical. He accuses President Bush of being "divisive"—but Obama began that very speech by openly ridiculing the President of the United States. Obama attacks and ridicules the sitting president, but if the President affirms American policy and defends it against *all* critics, Obama declares that the President has stepped over some imaginary ethical line.

Here's a clue, Mr. Obama: George W. Bush is not running for President, he *is* President. It is not divisive for the President to declare what American policy is and to defend it—that's his *job*.

If you don't want any divisiveness, Mr. Obama, then you will stop attacking American policy during wartime and stop promising that if you're elected, you will hand the victory over to our enemies.

If all the candidates of both parties had pledged their support for victory in Iraq and Afghanistan, then our battlefield success would translate into political success as well. Instead, because both [presidential candidate Hillary] Clinton and Obama have promised to surrender as soon as they are elected, they daily encourage our enemies to keep fighting, keep killing Americans, endure long enough for victory to be handed to them by the Democratic candidate.

Leave Foreign Policy to the President

This is why, for so many years, it was the policy of both parties to leave foreign policy *out* of election campaigns. Because when candidates for the job of commander-in-chief of the American military pledge to *withdraw* in the face of the enemy, regardless of whether we're winning or not, regardless of whether losing the war will have dire consequences—well, folks, that *is* direct interference with the President as he carries out his duties.

We reelected George W. Bush in the midst of this war. It was the will of the people in 2004 that Bush be allowed to run it for four more years. That's Democracy.

Obama and Clinton have spent many months now doing everything they can to undercut the duly-elected President and to subvert the accomplishments of our troops. By Obama's own admission, his policies are precisely the "appeasement" President Bush was warning against.

President Bush is not the one who is divisive. He is not the one who is out of line. He is the one who was elected to conduct American policy and who is leading American troops in war.

It is Obama who is divisively undercutting him at every step, Obama who is promising to give our enemies the enormous prestige and, yes, victory of sitting down with the American President without so much as hinting that they would give up terrorism against Americans or war against American troops.

It is almost hilarious that Obama accuses Bush of not playing fair by "attacking" Obama in a speech to a foreign parliament. It does not seem to occur to Obama that he has followed *no* rules of civility in his scorn and ridicule of our President, that he has followed no rules of patriotic support of American troops in his promise to undo all the accomplishments of our military.

Since Hillary Clinton has been every bit as stupid as Obama in her foreign policy declarations, we have to give her credit for having the brains *not* to put on the shoe and declare that it fits. Instead, she has sat back silently, letting Obama declare himself to be the appeaser that Bush was talking about.

Negotiation Is Surrender

Here's the political reality: If this election hinges on the war, John McCain will win it and the Democrat—whichever one it turns out to be—will lose. Americans hate to lose wars, and it will be easy to make the case that surrender in Iraq will promote terrorism everywhere—because it's the obvious truth.

In fact, we need our forward positions in Iraq because if Iran gets a nuke, we will have no choice but to destroy Iran's present government as quickly and ruthlessly as possible, precisely because they have stated their intention to use any such weapon to commit monstrous attacks against civilian populations.

On 23 August 1864, Abraham Lincoln seemed to be headed for electoral defeat at the hands of Democrat George McClellan, one of his more popular but less effective generals during the Civil War. McClellan, like Obama and Clinton, had already pledged to give up the war and declare defeat. He would "negotiate" with the Confederacy—which could only mean allowing the Confederacy to continue to exist, which would mean accepting the dissolution of the Union and the continuation of slavery. In short, it would have been complete defeat for the Union cause, and complete victory for the Confederacy. There was no other meaning that "negotiation" could have under those circumstances, and everybody knew it.

That is, of course, precisely what "negotiation" with terrorists and terrorist nations means today: If you negotiate with them, you have already accepted their right to exist *as terrorists*, and that means you have already lost the war because you have legitimized them.

The United States Must Negotiate with Hamas

Henry Siegman, interviewed by Bernard Gwertzman

Henry Siegman is a writer and journalist specializing in Middle East policy. He is a former senior fellow at the Council on Foreign Relations and former executive director of the American Jewish Congress and now directs the Middle East Project. Bernard Gwertzman is a consulting editor for publications of the Council on Foreign Relations. He is the former foreign affairs editor of the New York Times.

Hamas has the support of much of the Palestinian population. Therefore, there can be no peace between Israel and the Palestinians unless Hamas is included in negotiations. Israel and Hamas both seem willing to talk to each other. However, the George W. Bush administration opposes such negotiations because it falsely believes that Hamas is connected with al Qaeda. Therefore, no progress toward peace between Israel and Palestine is possible until a new U.S. president takes office in 2009.

G*wertzman: There's a bit of a lull right now in the fighting between Hamas and Israel, which has led to over one hundred dred Palestinians dead and a few Israelis in the past couple of weeks. Can you see a diplomatic way of getting a cease-fire that would permit peace talks to continue between Israel and the Palestinian Authority under [Palestinian party] Fatah leader, President Mahmoud Abbas?*

Henry Siegman, interviewed by Bernard Gwertzman, "Siegman: No Peace Possible Between Israel and Palestinians without Hamas," a CFR.org interview, March 7, 2008. Reproduced by permission. http:/www.cfr.org/publication/15683.

Siegman: I don't see talks between Israelis and Palestinians leading anywhere without finding a way of bringing Hamas—who constitute the government of roughly half the Palestinian people—into that process. You can't make peace with half the population and remain at war with the other half. The notion that the Israeli government leaders and our own government have that it is possible to exclude Hamas from peace talks and have a successful result from those talks is a fantasy. It's not going to happen.

The question is, is it possible to persuade the United States and Israel's government to allow Hamas to participate in this process?

The obvious question is, would Hamas participate even if it is allowed?

Well, let's go back in time a bit. After a Palestinian unity government was established in early 2007 as a result of the Mecca agreement, worked out by Saudi mediation, and even before that, when there were talks between Hamas and Fatah about the possibility of forming such a government, Hamas made it clear that though they themselves would not sit in on those discussions, they had no objections to such discussions proceeding or to Abbas, as the president of the Palestinian Authority and also the president of Fatah, conducting those negotiations. So there was no obstacle to the peace process going forward, particularly since Hamas committed itself to putting an agreement, if one was reached with Israel, to a public referendum. Also Hamas committed itself to abiding by the outcome of that referendum. The notion that you can't have peace talks while Hamas is in the government is simply not true.

U.S. Backed a Coup

Do you buy into this view that is in a new Vanity Fair *article that the United States planned, in cooperation with Fatah, to cause a coup in Gaza [territory disputed by Israel and Palestin-*

ians] and throw out Hamas, and that backfired, leading to the current split between Fatah and Hamas?

One does not need an investigative article to make that point to know it is true. The U.S. government made no secret whatsoever from the beginning that it intended to arm Abbas's security forces, appoint an American general to be in charge of that program, and provide finances for training, equipment, and the arming of these people. They said publicly the purpose of this project would be for these people to have a showdown with Hamas and to oust them from government. So, this was never a secret. This was always in the public domain.

I never saw that—that they were so blatant to say they wanted Fatah to oust Hamas.

Without Hamas's participation there is no way that Israel and [the Palestinian leadership] could reach agreement on . . . the major permanent-status issues.

Yes, they were precisely that blatant. What happened next is that under the direction of Mohammed Dahlan, who was Abbas's national security adviser, the Fatah militias in Gaza were instructed to attack Hamas forces and to create a sufficient level of anarchy that would allow Abbas's security forces to come in and to say they have to restore order and take over the government in Gaza. This never was a secret. In any event, the *Vanity Fair* article pretty much nails down the story.

When was this decision taken?

The decision, according to the article, was taken immediately after the election in January 2006. As the *Vanity Fair* story tells it, the State Department people and the White House were in a state of total shock when the election results came in.

Hamas was overwhelmingly elected and Fatah was ousted. Incidentally, at this time, Hamas itself was still observing a self-declared cease-fire. They were not sending in missiles or engaging in violence again Israel. I mention this because a lot of people are under the impression that this decision to overthrow Hamas is somehow related to Hamas' violence. That is simply not true. At the time this decision was taken, there was a cease-fire that Hamas had observed for a year and a half.

No Agreement Without Hamas

So given the current situation, a resumption of talks between Abbas and [Israeli] Prime Minister Ehud Olmert would result in really nothing, right?

It would result in nothing for essentially two reasons. First, both Israeli officials and American officials are not aware of what it is that Abbas can agree to. They see him as a moderate and he is a moderate in that he opposed the violence of the second intifada [uprising] in 2000, and always argued that this was not the way that Palestinians will achieve their national goal. But it is precisely because he has argued against violence that he is not in a position—particularly when he is at odds with Hamas—to make any kind of significant compromises in the Palestinian position. There is no way that Israelis will be able to get his agreement of what they consider to be their minimal red lines. That is one reason why without Hamas's participation there is no way that Israel and Abbas could reach agreement on the refugee issue, on the Jerusalem issue, and certainly not on the settlement and border issues, which comprise all of the major permanent-status issues.

The second reason is, . . . Hamas retains the capacity to blow up the negotiations at any point by simply engaging in violence. And if Hamas sees that there is a process going on that is intended to exclude them, to marginalize them, and ultimately to oust them, they are not going to allow the process to proceed.

Bush Is the Obstacle to Peace

The Bush administration will be out of office in ten months. The Israeli government is extremely weak because of a shaky coalition government. Both the U.S. and the Israeli governments won't deal with Hamas. How do you get over this? Do you wait until there is a new president?

There is no choice but to wait for a new president because on this precise issue of dealing with Hamas, without a resolution, no peace process can succeed. President Bush is not going to change his mind. At least that is what I am told by people who are in touch with him or talk to him about it. He is absolutely convinced that Hamas is part of the "Axis of Evil." He believes these are people who are essentially in the mold of al-Qaeda, that they support the globalist, jihadist ambition to take over the whole world and establish a caliphate [Islamic government], and so on.

Those convictions of Bush's are completely divorced from reality. The fact of the matter is that Hamas and al-Qaeda are totally at odds, and have been from the very beginning. Al-Qaeda doesn't believe in national liberation movements. They believe only in a religious return under a caliphate to the Islamic territories. The idea of a Palestinian nationalism, or any other, they reject completely. Al-Qaeda has no sympathy for Hamas and Hamas has publicly on several occasions repudiated and rejected the statements and prescriptions made by al-Qaeda's leaders for the Palestinian movement.

What about the Israelis? The Israelis know Hamas pretty well. When Hamas was in opposition to the PLO [Palestine Liberation Organization], the Israeli government had no great love for the PLO. Do you get any sense that the Israelis would like to deal with Hamas even though Hamas says it will never recognize the existence of the state of Israel?

Well, there was a poll recorded in *Haaretz* [an Israeli newspaper] that showed a majority of Israelis want their government to reach out to Hamas because they understand that you can't deal with the problem without Hamas' participation. Now there are some well-informed people who tell me that Olmert and others in his government were ready to deal with Hamas, were prepared to respond to Hamas's offer for a truce and to use the truce to allow a reestablishment of a unity government that would include Hamas and Fatah. But the opposition from Washington, from the White House, is so unyielding that they haven't been able to act on that.

Have you been following any of the American political campaigns? Have any of the candidates shown any interest in going beyond what the stated American policy is right now?

None of the candidates have said anything on the subject except the very bland, general statements that they are totally committed to the security of Israel. What their real positions are, if they have the responsibility in office to deal with the problem, I simply don't know.

There is not evidence . . . that [Hamas] accepted [Iran's] help on terms that make them subservient to Iran.

Some of the advisers to these people, if they remain influential advisers once they get into office, have views that are far less rigid, certainly quite different, than those held by Bush and his people. There will have to be a change in position eventually that not only allows but encourages Israeli leadership to bring Hamas into the process and to deal with the violence coming out of Gaza not militarily but diplomatically. But we're going to have to wait until the next administration.

Egypt and Iran

Do you think the Egyptians could work out a truce right now? The Egyptians are right now engaged in talking to Hamas about trying to work out a truce, acting as surrogate negotiators with Israel.

95

The Egyptians have played that role for some time now—with not very impressive results—since Gilad Shalit, the [Israeli] soldier who was kidnapped by some militant groups in Gaza a year and half ago. They have tried to formulate a package that would enable the parties to agree on a truce and to have an exchange of prisoners. So far, they simply have not been able to deliver. Whether they will be able to do so going forward is difficult to say, particularly since the situation has become even more complicated because there has been added to the mix the issue of the border between Egypt and Gaza. Israelis would like to see it resealed exactly the way it was before. That is something that is very difficult for Egypt to agree to since the Egyptians would then be seen as an accomplice in the Israeli effort to essentially strangle the population of Gaza. It is impossible at this point to cut a deal that doesn't address that issue as well.

Israelis have said more recently that Hamas has been using missiles made in Iran to hit Ashkelon [a city in Israel near Gaza]. Do you think that Iran is really involved now in helping out Hamas?

Hamas and Iran are not natural partners. Hamas are Sunnis [an Islamic sect]. Unlike the Hezbollah, who are Shiites [an Islamic sect, prevalent in Iran] and are natural partners with the Iranians, Hamas is not. Nevertheless, they are fighting, as they see it, for their survival. In those circumstances they will accept assistance from whoever will give it to them. The fact that they are Shiites will not prevent accepting their help. However, there is not evidence, as far as I know, that they have accepted that help on terms that make them subservient to Iran. When Iran tried to organize a meeting to protest the U.S.-sponsored Middle East peace conference [in late 2007], Hamas refused to attend, forcing the Iranians to cancel their plans.

Organizations to Contact

The editors have compiled the following list of organizations concerned with the issues presented in this book. The descriptions are derived from materials provided by the organizations. The list was compiled on the date of publication of the present volume; the information provided here may change. Be aware that many organizations take several weeks or longer to respond to inquiries, so allow as much time as possible.

American-Israeli Cooperative Enterprise (AICE)
2810 Blaine Drive, Chevy Chase, MD   20815
(301) 565-3918 • fax: (301) 587-9056
e-mail: mitchellbard@gmail.com
Web site: www.us-israel.org

AICE is a nonprofit, nonpartisan organization that seeks to strengthen the U.S.-Israeli relationship by developing social and educational programs that emphasize common values. AICE also works to enhance Israel's image by publicizing Israeli solutions to these problems. Its Web site includes numerous reports as well as the Jewish Virtual Library, a comprehensive online encyclopedia of Jewish history.

American Jewish Committee (AJC)
PO Box 705, New York, NY   10150
(212) 751-4000 • fax: (212) 891-1450
e-mail: pr@ajc.org
Web site: www.ajc.org

AJC is an international think tank and pro-Israel advocacy organization that works to strengthen U.S.-Israeli relations, build international support for Israel, and support the Israeli-Arab peace process. AJC's Web site contains links to breaking news stories, opinion surveys, and a wealth of AJC articles and publications, including, for example, the reports "Israel's Quest for Peace" and "Syria: Brokering Hate on Israel's Border."

Americans for Middle East Understanding (AMEU)
475 Riverside Drive, Room 245, New York, NY   10115-0245
(212) 870-2053 • fax: (212) 870-2050
e-mail: info@ameu.org
Web site: www.ameu.org

AMEU is an organization founded to foster a better understanding in America of the history, goals, and values of Middle
Eastern cultures and peoples, the rights of Palestinians, and
the forces shaping U.S. policy in the Middle EaStreet AMEU
publishes the *Link*, a bimonthly newsletter, as well as books
and pamphlets on the Middle EaStreet

Arab American Institute (AAI)
1600 K Street NW, Suite 601, Washington, DC   20006
(202) 429-9210 • fax: (202) 429-9214
e-mail: jzogby@aaiusa.org
Web site: www.aaiusa.org

The AAI represents the interests of Arab Americans in the
United States and serves as a resource for government officials, the media, political leaders, and others on public policy
issues that concern Arab Americans and U.S.-Arab relations.
The AAI Web site contains numerous links to articles about
the Middle East and its conflicts.

Foundation for Middle East Peace
1761 N Street NW, Washington, DC   20036
(202) 835-3650 • fax: (202) 835-3651
e-mail: info@fmep.org
Web site: www.fmep.org

The Foundation for Middle East Peace is a nonprofit organization that promotes a peaceful resolution of the Israeli-
Palestinian conflict. To do this, it sponsors programs and public speaking, makes small financial grants, and publishes the
bimonthly *Report on Israeli Settlements in the Occupied Territories*, which contains analysis and commentary on the Arab-
Israeli conflict.

Institute for Palestine Studies (IPS)

3501 M Street NW, Washington, DC   20007
(202) 342-3990 • fax: (202) 342-3927
e-mail: ipsdc@palestine-studies.org
Web site: www.palestine-studies.org

IPS is a private, nonprofit, pro-Arab institute unaffiliated with any political organization or government. Established in 1963 in Beirut, the institute promotes research, analysis, and documentation of the Arab-Israeli conflict and its resolution. IPS publishes quarterlies in three languages and maintains offices all over the world. The institute's U.S. branch publishes four quarterly journals in three languages, including the *Journal of Palestininan Studies* and the *Jerusalem Quarterly*, as well as numerous books and articles on the Arab-Israeli conflict and Palestinian affairs.

Middle East Forum

1500 Walnut Street, Suite 1050, Philadelphia, PA   19102
(215) 546-5406 • fax: (215) 546-5409
e-mail: info@meforum.org
Web site: www.meforum.org

The Middle East Forum is a think tank that works to define and promote American interests in the Middle EaStreet It supports strong American ties with Israel, Turkey, and other democracies as they emerge. It publishes the policy-oriented journal *Middle East Quarterly*, and its Web site includes articles, summaries of activities, and a discussion forum.

Middle East Institute

1761 N Street NW, Washington, DC   20036-2882
(202) 785-1141 • fax: (202) 331-8861
e-mail: mideasti@mideasti.org
Web site: www.mideasti.org

The Middle East Institute's mission is to promote better understanding of Middle Eastern cultures, languages, religions, and politics. It publishes numerous books, papers, audiotapes, and videos as well as the quarterly *Middle East Journal*.

Middle East Media Research Institute (MEMRI)
PO Box 27837, Washington, DC   20038-7837
(202) 955-9070 • fax: (202) 955-9077
e-mail: memri@memri.org
Web site: www.memri.org

MEMRI is a nonprofit, nonpartisan organization that trans-
lates and disseminates articles and commentaries from Middle
East media sources and provides analysis on the political,
ideological, intellectual, social, cultural, and religious trends in
the region.

Middle East Policy Council (MEPC)
1730 M Street NW, Suite 512, Washington, DC   20036-4505
(202) 296-6767 • fax: (202) 296-5791
e-mail: info@mepc.org
Web site: www.mepc.org

MEPC is a nonprofit educational organization founded in
1981 to promote a full discussion of issues affecting U.S.
policy in the Middle East for U.S. policy makers. It publishes
the quarterly journal *Middle East Policy*.

Middle East Research and Information Project (MERIP)
1500 Massachusetts Ave. NW, Suite 119
Washington, DC   20005
(202) 223-3677 • fax: (202) 223-3604
e-mail: ctoensing@merip.org
Web site: www.merip.org

MERIP is a nonprofit, nongovernmental organization established to provide information and analysis on the Middle East
to the media. It seeks to educate the public about the contem-
porary Middle East with particular emphasis on U.S. foreign
policy, human rights, and social justice issues. It publishes the
bimonthly *Middle East Report*.

U.S. Department of State, Bureau of Near Eastern Affairs

2201 C Street NW, Washington, DC   20520
(202) 647-4000
Web site: www.state.gov/p/nea

The Bureau of Near Eastern Affairs deals with U.S. foreign policy and U.S. relations with the countries in the Middle East and North Africa. Its Web site offers country information as well as news briefings and press statements on U.S. foreign policy.

Washington Institute for Near East Policy

1828 L Street NW, Suite 1050, Washington, DC   20036
(202) 452-0650 • fax: (202) 223-5364
e-mail: info@washingtoninstitute.org
Web site: www.washingtoninstitute.org

The institute is an independent, nonprofit research organization that provides information and analysis on the Middle East and U.S. policy in the region. It publishes numerous books, periodic monographs, and reports on regional politics, security, and economics, including *Policy Watch/Peace Watch*, which focuses on the Arab-Israeli peace process.

Bibliography

Books

Phyllis Bennis
Understanding the Palestinian-Israeli Conflict: A Primer. Northampton, MA: Olive Branch Press, 2007.

Ronen Bergman
The Secret War with Iran: The 30-Year Clandestine Struggle Against the World's Most Dangerous Terrorist Power. New York: Free Press, 2008.

John R. Bradley
Saudi Arabia Exposed: Inside a Kingdom in Crisis. Updated ed. New York: Palgrave Macmillan, 2005.

Jason Burke
Al-Qaeda: Casting a Shadow of Terror. New York: I.B. Tauris, 2003.

Rajiv Chandrasekaran
Imperial Life in the Emerald City: Inside Iraq's Green Zone. New York: Knopf, 2006.

Zaki Chehab
Inside Hamas: The Untold Story of the Militant Islamic Movement. New York: I.B. Tauris, 2007.

Simon Cottee and Thomas Cushman, eds.
Christopher Hitchens and His Critics: Terror, Iraq, and the Left. New York: New York University Press, 2008.

Alan Dershowitz
The Case for Israel. Hoboken, NJ: Wiley, 2003.

Seymour M. Hersh — *Chain of Command: The Road from 9/11 to Abu Ghraib.* New York: HarperCollins, 2004.

Alireza Jafarzadeh — *The Iran Threat: President Ahmadinejad and the Coming Nuclear Crisis.* New York: Palgrave, 2007.

Seth G. Jones and Martin C. Libicki — *How Terrorist Groups End: Lessons for Countering al Qa'ida.* Santa Monica, CA: Rand, 2008.

Baruch Kimmerling and Joel S. Migdal — *The Palestinian People: A History.* Cambridge, MA: Harvard University Press, 2003.

Michael T. Klare — *Blood and Oil: The Dangers and Consequences of America's Growing Petroleum Dependency.* New York: Metropolitan Books/Henry Holt, 2004.

John J. Mearsheimer and Stephen M. Walt — *The Israel Lobby and U.S. Foreign Policy.* New York: Farrar, Straus, and Giroux, 2007.

Augustus Richard Norton — *Hezbollah: A Short History.* Princeton, NJ: Princeton University Press, 2007.

Michael B. Oren — *Power, Faith, and Fantasy: America in the Middle East, 1776 to the Present.* New York: Norton, 2007.

George Packer — *The Assassins' Gate: America in Iraq.* New York: Farrar, Straus, and Giroux, 2005.

Barry Rubin — *The Truth About Syria.* New York: Palgrave Macmillan, 2007

Michael A. Sheehan	*Crush the Cell: How to Defeat Terrorism Without Terrorizing Ourselves.* New York: Crown, 2008.
Micah L. Sifry and Christopher Cerf, eds.	*The Iraq War Reader: History, Documents, Opinions.* New York: Touchstone Books, 2003.
Ray Takeyh	*Hidden Iran: Paradox and Power in the Islamic Republic.* New York: Times Books, 2006.

Periodicals

American Prospect	Special issue on the Middle East, June 2007.
Stephen Biddle, Michael E. O'Hanlon, and Kenneth M. Pollack	"How to Leave a Stable Iraq: Building on Progress," *Foreign Affairs*, September-October 2008.
Robert Bryce	"Oil for War," *American Conservative*, March 10, 2008.
Peter Coy	"Oil, Security, and Energy Independence," *BusinessWeek*, December 18, 2006.
Karen DeYoung	"Gates: U.S. Should Engage Iran with Incentives, Pressure," *Washington Post*, May 15, 2008.
Economist	"Can a Lull Be Turned into a Real Peace?" December 13, 2007.

Economist   "Larger-than-Life Diplomacy,"
                     November 6, 2008.

Economist   "Which War?" October 2, 2008.

James Fallows   "Will Iran Be Next?" *Atlantic*,
                     December 2004.

Jeffrey Goldberg   "Unforgiven," *Atlantic*, May 2008.

Yossi Klein Halevi   "The Iranian-Israeli War," *New
                     Republic*, March 2008.

Arthur Herman   "Why Iraq Was Inevitable,"
                     Commentary, July-August 2008.

Seymour Hersh   "Watching Lebanon," *New Yorker*,
                     August 21, 2006.

Richard   "The Longest War," *Washington Post*,
Holbrooke   March 31, 2008.

William Kristol   "Getting Serious About Syria," *Weekly
                     Standard*, December 20, 2004.

Daniel Levy   "The Next President and the Middle
                     East," *American Prospect*, April 2008.

Paul Marshall   "Egypt's Identity Crisis," *Weekly
                     Standard*, March 3, 2008.

Mark Mazzetti   "Amid U.S. Policy Disputes, Qaeda
and David Rohde   Grows in Pakistan," *New York Times*,
                     June 30, 2008.

Walter Russell   "The New Israel and the Old: Why
Mead   Gentile Americans Back the Jewish
                     State," *Foreign Affairs*, July-August
                     2008.

| Ron Moreau and Michael Hirsh | "Where the Jihad Lives Now," *Newsweek*, October 29, 2007. |

| Romesh Ratnesar et al. | "Al-Qaeda's New Home," *Time*, September 15, 2003. |

| David Rieff | "The Shiite Surge," *New York Times Magazine*, February 1, 2004. |

| Gabriel Schoenfeld | "Jews, Muslims, and the Democrats," *Commentary*, January 2007. |

| Ken Silverstein | "Jimmy Carter, Hamas, and the Media," *Harper's*, April 16, 2008. |

| Jason Lee Steorts | "The Ethical Case Against Withdrawal from Iraq," *National Review*, July 9, 2007. |

| Robert F. Worth and Nada Bakri | "Hezbollah Ignites a Sectarian Fuse in Lebanon," *New York Times*, May 18, 2008. |

Web Sites

Al Jazeera English (http://english.aljazeera.net/) Run by the Al Jazeera English language television channel based in Doha, Qatar. It provides a Middle Eastern perspective on both Middle Eastern and international events.

BBC News: Middle East (http://news.bbc.co.uk/2/hi/middle_east/default.stm). Run by the British Broadcasting Company and providing up-to-date news on Middle Eastern events.

Bitterlemons.org (www.bitterlemons.org). Presents Israeli and Palestinian viewpoints on the Palestinian-Israeli conflict and peace process as well as related regional issues of concern.

Global Connections (www.pbs.org/wgbh/globalconnections/ mideast/index.html). Provides timelines and background information about Middle Eastern geography, religion, culture, science, and politics.

Haaretz.com (www.haaretz.com/). An online edition of one of the leading Israeli newspapers published in English.

Islamic Republic News Agency (www2.irna.ir/en/). This agency of the government of Iran provides links to news articles and current affairs about that nation and the Middle East.

Mideast: Land of Conflict (www.cnn.com/SPECIALS/2003/ mideast/). Provides background information on the Arab-Israeli conflict.

MidEastWeb (www.mideastweb.org/) Founded by people from different nations who are active in peace education efforts, this site features articles and opinions about events in the region, as well as maps and a history of the conflict in the Middle East.

Index